small BIG GOD

8 Myths that Keep Christians in Bondage

Dr. Denver Cheddie

Indira Rampaul-Cheddie

small devil, BIG GOD: 8 Myths that Keep Christians in Bondage

Copyright © 2017 by Denver Cheddie and Indira Rampaul-Cheddie
All rights reserved. With the except of the use of brief quotations, no portion of this book may be reproduced or used in any manner whatsoever without the express written permission of the authors.

Copyright registered with the US Library of Congress
Registration number: TXu 2-054-513

ISBN-13: 978-1979119535
ISBN-10: 1979119538

BibleIssues.org

Unless otherwise stated, all scripture citations are taken from the NEW KING JAMES VERSION®, NKJV. Copyright© 1982 by Thomas Nelson, Inc. Used by permission. All rights reserved.

Scriptures marked KJV are taken from the KING JAMES VERSION (KJV), public domain.

Scriptures marked NIV are taken from the Holy Bible, New International Version®, NIV®. Copyright © 1973, 1978, 1984, 2011 by Biblica, Inc.™ Used by permission of Zondervan. All rights reserved worldwide. www.zondervan.com The "NIV" and "New International Version" are trademarks registered in the United States Patent and Trademark Office by Biblica, Inc.™

Scripture quotations marked RSV are from the Revised Standard Version Bible, copyright © 1946, 1952 and 1971 the Division of Christian Education of the National Council of the Churches of Christ in the United States of America. Used by permission. All rights reserved.

Scriptures marked NASB are taken from the NEW AMERICAN STANDARD BIBLE®, Copyright © 1960, 1962, 1963, 1968, 1971, 1972, 1973, 1975, 1977, 1995 by The Lockman Foundation. Used by permission.

Cover photo courtesy KT Design Studio (ktdesign9.wixsite.com/kiko). Used with permission.

To maintain a conversational tone, this book paraphrases commonly held beliefs and presents them as quotes by anonymous speakers. These are not direct quotes.

This book reports testimonies and experiences of individuals with their permission. However, to protect their privacy, names have been changed and details slightly modified without altering the gist of their stories.

The information in this book is meant to supplement; not replace personal devotion, prayer, Bible study and church attendance. The contents represent the authors' interpretations of the Bible, and are not intended as advice of any kind. The authors are not responsible for the decisions made by free citizens as a result of reading this book.

This book is dedicated to our natural, adopted and spiritual parents, whose sacrifices of love have contributed profoundly to our development and growth.

Ray, Phyllis, Gloria,
Vishpatie, Geita, Patsy,
Pastor Alonzo Jones, Pastor Stephen Mohammed,
Apostle Arnold Gajramsingh, Pastor Noreen Dottin,
and Pastor Wilma Kelly

We wish to acknowledge the various persons who helped in the writing of this book. Some of them took time off their busy schedules to volunteer reviews, critiques, feedback and editing services. We also thank those who offered their testimonies to be used in the book – John Dixon, Daniel Sawic, Suresh Boodoo, and the others (who preferred anonymity). We greatly appreciate their time and effort.

FOREWORD

On occasion when things don't seem to be going our way, we tend to give the devil too much credit. Quips such as, *"the devil made me do it"* or *"I have a demon following me today"* give an undue spotlight to Satan's influence. We may say these phrases flippantly and feel they are harmless quotes, but who is getting the glory: God or Satan? No matter how big or small the situation, the thing not to do is to give the devil his due.

"small devil, BIG GOD" tackles this everyday struggle that plagues so many believers. Authors Denver Cheddie and Indira Rampaul-Cheddie present eight common myths that arise from time to time, no matter how grounded we are in our faith. They dissect these myths and, addressing the spiritual and mental fallout that accompanies some of these myths, offer biblical alternatives to combat the devil's influence.

It's time to reaffirm our trust in the validity of scripture and less on myths, fables, and fairy tales.

DR. TIMOTHY M. HILL
General Overseer
Church of God International
Cleveland, TN

REVIEWS

In these days of great spiritual deception, false teaching, demonic possession and oppression, mankind is steeped in bondage and the traditions of men. This book *"small devil, BIG GOD"* is a welcome relief.

For those who really desire to study and practise the teachings of Jesus Christ and to understand His truths, light has come in great depth.

I have read and revised its contents and found it quite informative – enlightening to say the least – and great explanation and correction of myths and "old wives' tales" that have crippled our prayer-life and dwarfed our spiritual progress for centuries.

This book is an extensively, thoroughly and intellectually well-thought out bit of writing, as revealed by the inspiration of the Holy Spirit.

The main thread running through the book suggests that we should not add or take away from what the Lord God intends for our spiritual education. In other words, speak as God speaks or pray as Jesus taught us in Matthew 6:9 – *"When you pray say 'Our Father which art in heaven'"*.

This book is and will be very useful to the people of God now and in the future. It is an excellent piece of work presenting "truth" in a readable fashion that highlights the authors as knowledgeable, prominent personalities in the kingdom of God.

I highly recommend this book to the body of Christ.

PASTOR JOYCELYN NELSON
Woodbrook Pentecostal Church

This publication is a necessary contribution to the ongoing process of the exegetical work of Caribbean Christians as theologians who have had global encounters. The authors have drawn largely upon their own Christian journey experience by reconstructing and deconstructing the myths that enslave some Christians, especially some pastors and ministers of the gospel.

This impressively sized text moves from traditional exegesis-type work on specific texts in the Bible, through to more personal accounts of life experiences. I was impressed by the way in which the writers remind us that some Christian leaders can mislead their flock by their misinterpretation of biblical texts, especially in relation to the sovereignty and omnipotence of God and the devil's incapacity.

One of the strengths of the text is the way in which the authors show the means by which the Bible deconstructs the myths created by some leaders in the Caribbean and the world at large.

The text challenges Christians to develop a faith that seeks understanding through fervent prayer, critical faith thinking as well as wrestling with the text. The authors, in my view, challenge the status quo.

Albeit, this text reminds us of the fluidity and the imaginative flamboyance with which Caribbean biblical authors have engaged and wrestled with biblical and doctrinal texts on God and the devil. It definitely seeks to make the truth of the Gospel a lived reality rather than an 'unimaginable myth'.

REVEREND JOY ABDUL-MOHAN
Former Principal
St. Andrews Theological College

PREFACE

What if everything you believed turned out to be a lie, what would you do? Could you imagine how the Scribes, Pharisees, Sadducees and Chief Priests felt when Jesus burst on to the scene and turned their entire world upside down? Jesus was revolutionary. He was counter-culture. He was the kind of person you either love or hate. There was no in-between with Him. He totally dismantled the belief systems of the existing culture.

Jesus came to a world possessed by demons and yoked in bondage by religious traditions that made the common man slave to the powers-that-be. He did not care about political correctness or being nice. He came to set the captives free.

You can now experience for yourself how the Pharisees felt to have the rug yanked from under them. As you read this book, from the very first page, you will find your most cherished beliefs being challenged, disheveled and dismantled. (*Don't worry. We are not attacking any core Bible doctrine*). You will experience what the Pharisees felt, and you will probably understand why they hated Jesus so much, because you might just hate us too.

We are not asking you to give us an open mind. We are asking you to read with the intention of proving us wrong. Read with a pen and paper in hand. Write down every question you can think of, and every objection that comes up. We are that confident that as you read, every question will be answered, and every objection struck down.

But be prepared to be annoyed at first. You might hate us for writing this book. This book will challenge you. But if you believe the Bible is the Word of God, you will love us at the end. By the time you reach the last page, you will understand exactly why you needed to hear this message. You will understand why we wrote this book, and you will wonder why someone did not write this book years ago. You might even recommend it to your Christian friends.

Be blessed, be provoked, and be certain to search the scriptures for yourself to see if the things we say are really true.

TABLE OF CONTENTS

FOREWORD		iv
PREFACE		vii
INTRODUCTION		1
MYTH #1	I CAN DECREE MY BLESSINGS	11
Chapter 1	The new "Lord's Prayer"	12
Chapter 2	What the Bible says about decree-and-declare	21
MYTH #2	THE DEVIL IS HINDERING MY PRAYERS	26
Chapter 3	Do we have to take back what the devil stole?	27
Chapter 4	Am I under a generational curse?	35
MYTH #3	I NEED TO BIND THE DEVIL'S KINGDOM	40
Chapter 5	The true meaning of binding and loosing	41
Chapter 6	Do we have to bind the strongman?	48
MYTH #4	I THINK I HAVE A DEMON	56
Chapter 7	Can Christians have demons?	57
Chapter 8	Can witchcraft work against Christians?	64
MYTH #5	I CAN LAY LOW AND AVOID THE DEVIL	69
Chapter 9	Who is in control – God or the devil?	70
Chapter 10	Can we really avoid trials?	76
MYTH #6	THE DEVIL MADE ME DO IT	81
Chapter 11	What are strongholds?	82
Chapter 12	Testimonies of pulling down strongholds	87
MYTH #7	GOD IS ANGRY WITH ME	94
Chapter 13	Do we serve an angry God?	95
Chapter 14	Does sin give the devil access to us?	101
MYTH #8	I NEED TO TAP INTO THAT GOD PRINCIPLE	107
Chapter 15	Is there a secret prayer formula that moves God?	108
Chapter 16	Sow a seed, any seed, act now!	115
CONCLUSION		122
REFERENCES		126
ABOUT THE AUTHORS		127

INTRODUCTION

Do you feel like a bird in a cage?

One of my new-found joys in life is waking early and sitting on the porch with my morning cup of coffee. I particularly enjoy watching the birds fly by. My rural neighborhood is populated with many varieties of birds – blackbirds, herons, parrots, parakeets – and even woodpeckers and hummingbirds. They come in all sizes and colors, each flying in coordinated choreography, singing in perfect harmony. What makes this such an enjoyable pastime is the fact that these birds are free. They look happy, and they get to be the way birds were created to be – free.

I hate seeing birds in cages. They look depressed and borderline suicidal. I wonder if they were once free and then captured, or if they were born in captivity. Is captivity all they ever knew? I wonder if they even realize they are not free. I think deep down, they suspect that something is not right. That is not how God created them to be.

Many Christians are like birds in a cage. They are in bondage and don't even realize it. As I am writing this, I am thinking about the many Christians I know who have struggled with sickness for a long time. This in itself is not necessarily bondage. But they have prayed and prayed and nothing has changed. They have gone to faith healer after faith healer, deliverance minister after deliverance minister ... and still sick. They have gone to Benny Hinn crusades, Morris Cerullo conferences ... and nothing. They have been *"slain in the spirit"* by the most *"anointed"* preachers in history, yet every time they got back up sick.

Then someone told them to start confessing the Word. So they printed out all the healing scriptures and confessed them daily like a mantra. Then they heard someone on TV say, *"No it's not confession anymore, it's declaration. You need to start declaring your healing."* So they started declaring, although in their honest moments, they could not for the life of them figure out the difference between declaring and confessing. Then someone else told them, *"You don't need to pray for healing, you are already healed. By His stripes you <u>were</u> healed. Your symptoms are a lie of the devil."*

The cumulative effect of this colossal runaround is utter confusion, dejection and rejection. They are not sure if they should go to the doctor or if that is a sign they don't have faith. They are not even sure how to pray anymore. <u>They are in bondage not because of their sickness, but because of all the crazy weird doctrines they have been taught</u>. They have been drained of all peace, and their joy has been stifled out of them. They are like birds in a cage. They are in bondage because they have been fed a diet of myths rather than truth.

Beware of myths and fables

> *...you shall know the truth, and the truth shall make you free ... (John 8:32)*
>
> *...if the Son makes you free, you shall be free indeed ... (John 8:36)*

The Bible declares that who the Son sets free is free indeed, but it also says that we shall know the truth and the truth shall set us free. Putting the two together, we can surmise that Jesus sets His people free by revealing truth to them.

If you are in Christ, then Jesus has set you free from the penalty of the law and from the punishment of eternal damnation. But there are other aspects of your life where you may not experience that freedom because you don't know the truth. And it's not just lack of knowledge that's destroying you, it's believing the wrong things. There are two opposites of knowing the truth:
1) Not knowing the truth (*ignorance*)
2) Believing something that's not true (*deception*)

You can be ignorant or you can be deceived, either way the devil has you bound and you may not even realize it. Paul warned Timothy and Titus there would be many people in the last days preaching myths and fables.

> ... command certain people not to teach *false doctrines* any longer or to devote themselves to *myths* and endless genealogies... (1 Timothy 1:3-4, NIV, emphasis mine)
>
> ... Have nothing to do with godless *myths* and old wives' *tales*... (1 Timothy 4:7, NIV, emphasis mine)
>
> ... avoiding the profane and idle *babblings* and contradictions of what is falsely called knowledge... (1 Timothy 6:20, emphasis mine)
>
> But shun profane and idle *babblings*, for they will increase to more ungodliness... (2 Timothy 2:16, emphasis mine)
>
> They will turn their ears away from the truth and turn aside to *myths*... (2 Timothy 4:4, NIV, emphasis mine)
>
> For there are many insubordinate, both *idle talkers* and *deceivers*... rebuke them sharply, that they may be sound in the faith, not giving heed to Jewish *fables* and *commandments of men* who turn from the truth... (Titus 1:10, 13-14, emphasis mine)

Even though ours is a generation where knowledge has increased, somehow Christians are more ignorant and deceived than ever before. On one hand it is a knowledge generation, on the other hand it is an itching-ears generation. Knowledge is out there, yet Christians prefer to believe myths because they are more pleasing to the ears, not realizing they are deceitfully crippling to the soul.

If knowing truth sets you free, then logically not knowing truth or believing myths has the opposite effect. Myths work to keep you in bondage. And because myths are so deceptive, you don't realize you're in bondage. You are like the bird in the cage. You are like Bruce Willis in *The Sixth Sense*. He was dead all along and didn't even know it. This is an apt description of the Laodiceans. They thought they were healthy, wealthy and wise, but Jesus said they were wretched, miserable, poor, blind, and naked (*Revelation 3:17*). They were obviously deceived. Interestingly, many Bible scholars believe the Laodiceans refer to the end-time church.

Myths make our prayers ineffective

Now not all myths are created equal. Some myths are so ridiculous, they are laughable. For example, when a well-known TV preacher said that the Greek word for rejoice means to leap, spin in a circle and shout; you just have to laugh at that. But there are some myths that are detrimental and can diminish the very effectiveness of our prayers.

One of my favorite movies is *Taken*. There is a scene at the end of the movie where Liam Neeson's character, Brian, confronts Jean-Claude, his long-time friend-turned-nemesis. During the encounter, Jean-Claude pulls out his gun, not realizing that Brian had earlier removed the bullets. That's what the devil's myths have done to us – they have taken the bullets out of our gun and rendered our prayers ineffective.

Have you fallen prey to any of his myths? How effective are your prayers? Why don't you take the prayer quiz below to test yourself? Although this is not a scientific test, it is a fun quiz and might reveal a lot about how effective your prayers are.

QUIZ: How effective are you prayers?

Answer these 10 questions as honestly as you can. You can also take it online at www.bibleissues.org/biblequiz to get your results. Feel free to share with your friends on social media.

1. How do you pray for someone with a back pain?
    a. I bind the spirit of back pain in Jesus' name!
    b. Be healed in Jesus' name!
    c. Lord please heal this person's back
    d. Lord, I know that you stopped healing 1926 years ago, so I am asking you to give this person strength to endure this back pain for Jesus. You can empathize with their pain Lord, because I'm pretty sure your back hurt when you carried that heavy cross. Give us strength to carry our cross for you.

2. How do you pray for courage?
    a. I cast out the spirit of fear in Jesus' name!
    b. I decree and declare that I am bold and courageous!
    c. Lord, you did not give me a spirit of fear. Give me soundness of mind and take away all fear so I can face this situation with the same boldness as Christ himself.
    d. Lord please give me courage

3. How do you pray for a husband / wife?
    a. Here is a list of what I want in a husband/wife Lord, I visualize it into being right now, in Jesus' name
    b. Lord please guide me in my search for a husband/wife, and give me wisdom to make the best choices
    c. Lord please send someone ... anyone
    d. Lord, I'm waiting. When will you send me a husband/wife? Why me Lord? Why?

4. How do you pray for your unsaved loved ones?
    a. Lord, put a hook in their jaw and pull them in.
    b. Lord, as I share the gospel with them, I pray for conviction by the Spirit.
    c. Lord, save them.
    d. Lord, I know you will save whom you will save, so if it is your will to save them please do so, if not, let them rot in hell, in Jesus' name.

5. How do you pray for your pastor?
    a. I anoint him in Jesus' name.
    b. Lord, give him a shepherd's heart that he will continue to selflessly feed your flock.
    c. Lord, I pray for my pastor. Remember him Lord.
    d. Lord, please help him to not be boring this Sunday.

6. How do you pray for financial prosperity?
    a. I decree and declare that I am rich, and that the seed I sowed to the TV preacher Reverend Get-Rich-Quick will multiply 30-fold, 60-fold, 100-fold, 1 gazillion-fold
    b. Lord bless the work of my hands and cause what I do to prosper. Give me the power to get wealth.
    c. Lord supply my needs according to your riches in glory.
    d. Lord I want to be poor. It is your will for Christians to be poor, so please take stuff away from me.

7. How do you pray for your country?
    a. I claim this land for Jesus by the authority of God Almighty
    b. Lord I pray for our political leaders that you will lead them to Christ, so we can live peaceable lives
    c. Lord I pray for my country
    d. Lord, I cannot pray against Bible prophesy. Things will get worse and worse. Please let the rapture take place right now.

8. How do you pray for favor?
    a. I am blessed and highly favored, amen
    b. Lord teach me mercy and truth so I can find favor with God and man
    c. Lord please give me favor
    d. Lord, I don't care about favor with the world. I only want favor with you.

9. How do you pray for God's will to be done?
    a. I speak God's will into existence on earth as it is in heaven
    b. Lord I pray that you will keep me in your perfect will and not let me stray. Holy Spirit, lead me.
    c. Lord, let your will be done on earth as it is in heaven.
    d. Lord, whatever happens is your will.

10. How do you pray for forgiveness for sin?
    a. I confess that I am the righteousness of God in Christ Jesus
    b. Lord, I have sinned. This is what I did, please forgive me and cleanse me with your blood.
    c. Lord please forgive me for my sins.
    d. Lord it does not matter whether I confess my sins or not, I am the elect of God so I will go to heaven regardless. Amen.

Take the quiz online at www.bibleissues.org/biblequiz to get your results.

God-limiting myths

Would you go to war using weapons that your enemy gave you? Then why do we engage in spiritual warfare using prayer techniques that are found nowhere in the Bible?

Do you spend more of your prayer time binding the devil than actually communing with God? Do you use the phrase *"decree and declare"* when you pray even though NO ONE in the Bible prayed like that? Do you focus on trying to take back what the devil stole rather than simply asking God to supply your daily bread? Or perhaps, when you do pray to God, do you spend most of your time on your own needs and wants as if God were some kind of deified Santa Claus? Were you taught that you should just pray once for a need, because God does not want you to ask for the same thing over and over? Do you think your prayers are not being answered because God hates you or is angry with you or because of some demon in your life?

If you answered yes to any of those questions, you have believed myths rather than truth. This is more than just an academic issue. The myths I am talking about are not merely intellectual untruths amounting to nothing more than incorrect answers on a trivia quiz. These are myths that affect how we pray. They affect our very understanding of God. These are what I refer to as God-limiting myths. By our own crazy beliefs, we limit the God to whom we pray. These myths keep us in bondage, and keep our prayers from being answered.

<u>Without realizing it, many Christians believe in a big devil and a small god</u>. They obviously won't come out openly and say that. But listen to how they speak. Listen to how they pray. Why do you feel the need to *"take back what the devil stole"?* Obviously your god is so small, that when he gives something, the devil bullies him and takes it away, and *"god"* can't do anything about it. Why do you need to keep binding the devil instead of praying to God to deliver us from the evil one? It's because your god is so small that you have to do his job for him. Or maybe if you and god team up, maybe you stand a chance of defeating the devil.

Notice how I keep using a lower case *"g"* for god, because that god is not the God of the Bible. The God of the Bible is big. Satan is a defeated foe. Compared to God, he is small. We make the devil bigger than he really is. We magnify him in our minds because of God-limiting myths that we believe and don't even realize it.

<u>How the devil undermines our prayers</u>

Although the devil is small in power and authority, he is very cunning and crafty. He can be considered a little genius. Because of God's hedge around us, he can't touch Christians, however he is a manipulative little master at getting us to destroy ourselves. One of his strategies is planting myths that undermine our prayer lives. Prayer is one of the most powerful weapons in the Christian's arsenal, so the devil seeks to dull our big weapons.

If I were the devil's strategic advisor, here is how I would attack Christians' prayer lives. I would search their own scriptures for verses on prayer, for example:

The effective, fervent prayer of a righteous man avails much… (James 5:16)

I find in that verse three ingredients for powerful availing prayer:
    1) righteousness, 2) fervency and 3) effectiveness.

Then I would formulate a strategy around that. The first thing I would do is send temptations so Christians would sin and experience condemnation whenever they stand before God in prayer. The second thing I'd do is send distractions to either make them not pray or pray half-heartedly or perfunctorily, without any real passion or fervency.

If that does not work, there is still one more thing I can do. According to James 5:16, even if a righteous man prays fervently, that is not enough. His prayer must also be effective in order to avail much. My final strategy would be to send deceptions and false teachings that would cause Christians to pray ineffectively.

We pray, we bind, we loose, we call down fire from heaven – and we think we are so powerful – but nothing happens. We are like a car with a broken muffler – loud but devoid of any real power. Pastors pray for the same people over and over, yet nothing ever changes in their lives. Everyone falls down but no one gets healed.

Sure the believers themselves may lack faith, but they are obviously not being equipped with freedom-setting truth. You can't be set free by having hands laid on you, you must be taught the truth. Are you satisfied with blaming people for their lack of faith, or does it seem like a cop-out? Do you think, that just maybe, the devil has planted myths that are contributing to our powerlessness? Do you think that maybe the devil has planted myths that contribute to people's lack of faith?

If you are too quick to accept and embrace every new teaching you hear, then you probably do not believe the Bible when it says,

> *Now the Spirit expressly says that in latter times some will depart from the faith, giving heed to deceiving spirits and doctrines of demons...(1 Timothy 4:1)*

If you were the devil's strategic advisor, where would you plant those false teachers? Wouldn't you place them in the most influential pulpits in the Christian world? Wouldn't you plant them on Christian TV, Christian radio and Christian magazines? Then why do you assume that the devil has not already done this?

How this book can help you

Do you sometimes feel that living the Christian life is hard work? Does it seem as though your yoke is <u>not</u> easy and your burden is <u>not</u> light? We put it to you that the myths we have identified in this book have the effect of making your Christian walk tiring and fraught with burdens that God never meant for us to carry. As you continue to read this book ... after the initial feeling of resistance has worn off ... you will slowly feel these burdens being lifted, and you will enjoy the freedom that truth brings.

We will show you in this book that the devil has planted numerous God-limiting myths that are keeping us in bondage and rendering our prayers ineffective. Your prayers are not working because of God-limiting myths you don't even know you believe. Here are some of the myths we will debunk:

- I need to bind the devil in order for God to give me the victory.
- It is my job to take back what the devil stole.
- If I pray in my mind, the devil can't hear me and therefore he won't attack me.
- The devil made me do it.
- I need deliverance from demons.
- I need deliverance from witchcraft.
- God is angry with me.
- I am under a generational curse.
- If I sow a seed, God will bless me.
- God does not want to hear me praying over and over for the same thing. I will just pray once, and then thank God for the answer.

Talk about God-limiting myths that betray a belief in a small god and a big devil! Talk about bondage! These myths are slave masters to the ones who believe them. Not only will we expose these myths, but we will show you the truth of scripture. We will show you how the Bible teaches us to pray – for ourselves, for our unsaved loved ones, for healing, deliverance, protection and many other issues we face. We will share some of our own experiences and testimonies. We will also share how some of the members of our *Bible Issues* Facebook group used the truth of God's Word to overcome lust, fear, unforgiveness, and generally to escape bondage.

These truths may not be popular, and may in some cases run totally against the grain of contemporary Christian culture, but modern Christian culture often runs contrary to the Word of God. If you are accustomed to playing with an empty gun, a loaded gun will feel heavy. Changing your diet and exercising will never feel good if you're accustomed to living unhealthily. Similarly if mythology is deeply ingrained in your theology, the truth is going to be very uncomfortable.

Nevertheless if you're interested in truth, this book is for you. If you are interested in learning to pray effectively, this book is for you. We cannot guarantee that God will answer your every prayer because there is something called the sovereignty of God that is bigger than you and I. We have no formula that is guaranteed to move the hand of God. Anyone who claims to have that is a presumptuous myth-propagator. But you can learn to pray effectively, and in so doing, you can experience more of the freedom that Christ has ordained for His people.

If you have listened to a lot of Christian TV, and you are not comfortable with all these new make-shift teachings, then this book is for you. You probably know deep-down inside that something is just not right with these teachings. But perhaps you think they are harmless and are unaware of how negatively they impact your Christian walk. You will find this book liberating, not because we are such great writers, but because the truths that we reveal are all in scripture. These are the truths that can set you free.

We will demonstrate over and over that the devil is small, although Christians have made him bigger than he really is. We will demonstrate that our God is big, although many have limited Him and made Him small. We will show you how a scriptural revelation of the bigness of God can help you overcome a lot of the spiritual bondage you face.

When we decided to write this book, we prayed to God for a message that is relevant to Christians today. We did not just want to produce an intellectually correct document, but a book with a message that will help Christians live victoriously through Biblical truth.

We subsequently went through a series of experiences where we had no choice but to trust in the bigness of our God. I am talking about experiences like being stranded on a freezing cold night in a deserted part of South Africa without a vehicle or a working cell phone. There were signs not too far away that read *"HIGH CRIME AREA: beware of car-jackings and armed robberies"*. I picked up a stone from the ground and put in my pocket just in case I needed to use it as a weapon. We had no clue how to get back to our hotel, and we were scared. We did the only thing we could do – pray.

Then a security guard showed up, who turned out to be a born-again Christian, and called a taxi for us. I was certain that if I had looked back to wave goodbye, the security guard would no longer be there, because it felt as though he was an angel rather than an actual human being. It was clear that God was teaching us through these experiences, that *"small devil, Big God"* was not just a Bible study, but real life.

We pray that God will be magnified in your life when you are finished with this book. We pray that *"Big God"* will also define your Christian experience. Congratulations on starting your journey towards freedom.

MYTH #1

I CAN DECREE MY BLESSINGS

How this myth keeps us in bondage

This is a myth that makes God small and ourselves big. It overestimates the authority that Christ has given us, and because of this, we speak to our circumstances rather than actually pray to God. Because we are presuming authority that belongs to God alone, our prayers are based on pride rather than humility before God. God resists the proud, so our prayers are rendered ineffective.

What you will learn in the next two chapters

- The numerous problems associated with the doctrine of decree-and-declare
- How it keeps Christians in bondage
- What authority Christ has actually given us
- What the Bible says about decree-and-declare
- The right way to make declarations in our prayer

Let the truth free you from the burden of believing that anyone can speak words against you and steal your blessings. Let the truth free you from the burden of trying to exercise authority you do not have, and then wondering why it's not working.

CHAPTER 1

THE NEW "LORD'S PRAYER"

Our Father, we DECREE and DECLARE that Thou art in heaven, for had we not done so, Thou mightest have fallen from heaven like lightning

We CONFESS by faith that Your Name is hallowed

We CALL forth your kingdom, and we SPEAK your will on earth as in heaven

We DECLARE that we are rich and not poor

RELEASE forgiveness to us as we RELEASE forgiveness to others

We RESIST temptations, and we BIND the evil one in Jesus' name

We acknowledge that Thine is the kingdom, we assign to you power, and we give you the glory, Amen.

The first thing you will notice about this satirical version of the Lord's Prayer is that it is totally different from the one in the Bible – you know that old book with cobwebs on it. Jesus taught us to pray one way, and we decided *"Hey let's totally disregard what He said and do our own thing."*

The second thing to notice is that it is not a prayer at all. It is not asking for anything. There is no dependence on God. In fact, it seems to shift all the focus to us and our authority. If you attend a Charismatic church, watch Christian TV or listen to Christian radio, you would hear similar *"prayers"* all the time. You could attest that I did not exaggerate or misrepresent in any way. This is actually the new way to pray in Charismatic circles.

Do you pray this way because everyone else is doing it? Do you *"speak into the lives"* of your unsaved loved ones rather than actually pray for them? Are you OK with gambling their salvation on a new way of praying that is not even in the Bible? Or deep down inside, do you feel something is just not right with this new teaching? Remember at the beginning of this book, I mentioned that a key strategy of the devil is to pervert our prayers.

Whenever something new comes along, you have to seriously and honestly question whether it is a new move of the Holy Spirit, or an old lie of a seducing spirit. This is serious business. This is where the rubber meets the road. Are you praying to God, or are you trying to become God yourself? Have you fallen for Satan's oldest lie *"You shall be like God" (Genesis 3:5)*?

The Bible says that God resists the proud, but gives grace to the humble *(James 4:6)*. Are you humbling yourself before God or are you assigning to yourself authority that belongs to God alone. That could be a form of pride, and it could be a reason why God seems to be resisting your prayers. I will show you that *"decree-and-declare"* is not just unscriptural, it also presumes authority that God never gave us. Because of this, it is a form of pride that compromises our prayers before God.

Before you rise up in holy indignation and burn this book, let me ask you a question. How many things have you decreed and declared that have come to pass? How many have <u>not</u> come to pass? Perhaps you're not making your voice sound deep and authoritative enough. If this type of prayer is so effective, then why are so many of your decrees and declarations not manifesting into reality? OK it was three questions.

What is "decree-and-declare"?

Decree-and-declare is the latest incarnation of the Word of Faith movement. It is an offshoot of Positive Confession theology – name it and claim it, confess it and possess it, blab it and grab it. It teaches that Christians have the authority to decree things in the spiritual realm, which one author describes as causing things in the spiritual realm to manifest in the earthly realm.[1] Then we can declare it in our lives. They tend to treat the terms decree and declare as a single synonymous action, although technically they mean different things.

Here is an excerpt from *thechurchguide.com* on how to make breakthrough prayers by decreeing and declaring. Notice how similar they are to the parodied Lord's Prayer at the beginning of this chapter.

> *I decree my children shall be for signs and wonders. They shall walk in obedience*
>
> *I decree that my children will have personal intimate relationships with God, and the fear of the Lord will be evident in their daily walk with God*
>
> *I declare by faith that Jesus will supply all my needs, spiritually, financially, physically and emotionally throughout this year*
>
> *I declare that God will enrich my life with the abundance of His joy*

> *I declare that the power, glory and the kingdom of the living God will come upon every aspect of my life, in the name of Jesus* [2]

Now I don't have a problem with declarations per se. Declare is simply an English word that means to say or tell. The Psalms are full of declarations of God's faithfulness, greatness and majesty. Here are three examples.

> *I will tell of all your marvelous works ... (Psalm 9:1)*
>
> *The heavens declare the glory of God ... (Psalm 19:1)*
>
> *The Lord is my light and my salvation; whom shall I fear? The Lord is the strength of my life; of whom shall I be afraid? ... (Psalm 27:1)*

Those are declarations. Scriptural declarations are perfectly in order. Declarations based on the authority of God's Word are scriptural. Declarations of God's greatness are strongly encouraged in our prayer. However, self-centered declarations such as *"I declare that I shall have 4 houses and 6 cars"* are not scriptural.

As we peruse the scriptures, we find that decreeing is the real problem. I will show you that God never gave Christians the authority to decree. Decreeing is only something that God can do. I will demonstrate that decreeing is based on a misunderstanding or overstatement of the authority that God has given us. Hence when we decree, we are actually usurping God's authority and exhibiting pride before Him. I will also demonstrate that the scriptures do not teach that we can decree, neither is there a single person who prayed this way in the Bible. *"Decree-and-declare"* is a myth that makes God small and ourselves big.

Decree-and-declare is not prayer

> *Be anxious for nothing, but in everything by prayer and supplication, with thanksgiving, let your requests be made known to God ... (Philippians 4:6)*

Today there are people decreeing and declaring around the clock, yet not praying at all. They are talking to their problems but not talking to their God. They are not asking, and James 4:2 said we do not have because we do not ask. The Bible teaches that we should ask, seek and knock – all of which display dependence and trust in God. Decree-and-declare is all about us. I dare say your prayers are not working because you spend too much time decreeing and declaring instead of humbly making your petitions known to God.

Decree-and-declare – the new spiritual

I remember praying once on the radio, and someone called in and congratulated me for the spiritual growth they had noticed in me. I was really flattered, I almost blushed. But how did they know that I had grown spiritually? Is it because I no longer get angry when I lose at Scrabble? Is it because I no longer consider it a personal offense when someone cuts me off in traffic? Did they notice more of the fruit of the Spirit in my life?

No. It was none of that. The person thought I had grown because they heard me make declarations in my prayer. Now I am pretty sure they heard wrong because I don't follow these new doctrines. I pray the way the Bible teaches us to pray. I am certainly not into this declaration thing.

But then I started thinking, since when did making declarations in prayer become a sign of spiritual maturity and growth? 1 Timothy 3 gives a long list of things that measure spiritual maturity – we should be blameless, temperate, sober-minded, well-behaved, hospitable, not drunkards, not violent, not greedy, not quarrelsome, not covetous. Making declarations in prayer is not one of them. Far from being a measure of maturity, decree-and-declare has actually had the opposite effect on Christians.

These doctrines produce weird and fearful Christians

A friend of ours, who is a medical doctor, called one day asking for prayer.

"Please pray with me. My coworker is pronouncing curses on me."

Immediately we sprang into action. Like President George W. Bush after 9/11, we were ready for war. However we needed some clarification first. How exactly was this coworker pronouncing curses?

"She [the coworker] told me that I could get sued for how I handled a particular patient at work."

We waited a few seconds for her to continue with the rest of the story. There was no rest of the story. That was it. The coworker told her she could get sued because of how she handled a situation at work, and she interpreted that as pronouncing curses.

On another occasion, I was at the airport with two friends waiting for a connection. One of them told us about a time he missed his connecting flight because of a tight layover. After he left, the other friend whispered to me, *"We will NOT miss our connection. I cancel those curses in Jesus' name."*

This is the logical effect of positive confession theology. It makes us weird and unbearable. It also makes us fearful of words – ours and other people's. Are words bigger than the God you serve? Is God so small that words in casual conversation can remove His blessings and protection from us?

Perhaps you have had similar experiences. Perhaps you know certain Christians you can't even have a conversation with because of this. They can't even answer simple questions like:

How are you?

> *I am blessed and highly favored!*

But how do you feel?

> *I walk by faith and not feelings!*

And how is your back? I know you had some back pains recently.

> *I am healed in Jesus' name. With His stripes I AM HEALED!!!*

But you appear to be walking with a limp.

> *STOP PRONOUNCING CURSES ON ME!*

Talk about being a weirdo. Talk about walking in fear. I know someone else who is heavily involved in Word of Faith theology. One of her unsaved neighbors confided in her that he was terminally ill and probably was not going to live through the weekend. She rebuked him for confessing those words. *"Don't say that you are going to die. You will live and will not die!"* A normal Christian would have made sure to share the gospel with the guy, considering that people nearing their death tend to be more open to the gospel. The guy died the next day.

This is how you know a theology is flawed. It causes you to live unscriptural lives. By her actions, she valued the doctrine of positive confession/declaration more than the great commission.

Did Paul decree and declare?

If you have been saved for over 10 years, you would agree that *"decree-and-declare"* is a relatively new thing. Before 2005, nobody prayed using that terminology. That alone is sufficient to discredit it as a Biblical doctrine. The Bible is old. The church of Jesus Christ is 2000 years old. It has gone through trials, persecutions, Bible burnings, the Dark Ages. Yet it has survived every time. Are you so presumptuous to think you are going to discover something in the Bible that no one in the history of the world has ever seen? Come on, be real. Chances are that any new revelation is going to be from a seducing spirit rather than the Holy Spirit. This alone should discredit *"decree-and-declare"*.

If you look at the decree-and-declare *"prayers"* that I quoted earlier, you would notice that they are totally different from how people prayed in the Bible. You will not find a single example of anyone in the Bible praying using this verbal formula *"I decree and declare ..."* One of the best ways to test any new thing is to ask the following questions:

- Did Jesus do it?
- Did Paul do it?
- Did Peter do it?
- Did any reputable person in the Bible (*especially the New Testament*) do it?
- And if not, why on earth are we doing it?

You will also find that no one in the Bible was overly cautious of saying the wrong words when they prayed or spoke. Read the words of Jesus and Paul, and tell me if you think they believed in positive declarations.

> *Then He [Jesus] said to them, "My soul is exceedingly sorrowful, even to death ... (Matthew 26:38, emphasis mine)*

> *But I [Paul] fear, lest somehow, as the serpent deceived Eve by his craftiness, so your minds may be corrupted from the simplicity that is in Christ ... For I fear lest, when I come, I shall not find you such as I wish ... (2 Corinthians 11:3; 12:20, emphasis mine)*

"Decree-and-declare" misunderstands the believer's authority

You would also notice that the decree-and-declare *"prayers"* address things that God clearly teaches us to pray for, but instead of praying for God to give us health and prosperity, it decrees and declares that we are healthy and prosperous. Decree-and-declare takes all of the emphasis away from God and places it on ourselves. Consider the following two prayers:

> *"I decree and declare that I will be successful in my business ventures"*

> *"Lord, if it is your will, give me success in my business ventures"*

Decree-and-declarists prefer to pray the first way because it sounds more authoritative. But this is very misleading. Sounding authoritative and being authoritative are two entirely different things. The second prayer is more scriptural, and there is no higher authority on earth than God's Word. Compare it with James 4:15,

Instead you ought to say, "If the Lord wills, we shall live and do this or that." ... (James 4:15)

Further, authority has very little to do with our choice of words. Authority is based on who we are and who we represent, not what we say. A homeless guy can shout at you to stop, that means absolutely nothing. A police officer does not even have to use words to tell you to stop. All he has to do is raise his hand or point at you, and you immediately recognize his authority and you stop. Authority does not reside in our words, but in God's Word. Therefore, when you pray, you don't have to be too conscious about your choice of words. In fact, God knows what you need before you even utter a single word. Just talk with Him.

God has given us some authority

Decree-and-declare attributes more authority to Christians than what God has actually given us. When it comes to the believer's authority, there are two extremes to avoid. One extreme is to minimize our authority in Christ. Here are three scriptures that clearly teach that Christ has given us authority.

And these signs will follow those who believe: In My name they will cast out demons; they will speak with new tongues; they will take up serpents; and if they drink anything deadly, it will by no means hurt them; they will lay hands on the sick, and they will recover ... (Mark 16:17-18)

... he who believes in Me, the works that I do he will do also; and greater works than these he will do, because I go to My Father ... (John 14:12)

Behold, I give you the authority to trample on serpents and scorpions, and over all the power of the enemy, and nothing shall by any means hurt you ... (Luke 10:19)

We clearly have been given authority over demons and sickness. Some argue that the Mark scripture is not part of the original Bible. But even so, there is no textual dispute over John 14:12. Those who believe in Christ are expected to do the same works that Christ did and greater. Jesus raised us up to sit with Him in heavenly places above principalities and power, and He gave us authority over the devil's power. Christ has definitely given us authority.

Once I was part of a deliverance session and the demon-possessed guy started lunging toward me doing perfectly executed Karate kicks and punches – even though the individual who was possessed never took a Karate class in his life. I commanded the demon, *"Be crippled in Jesus' name!"* and the man immediately stopped in his tracks and fell to the ground. This allowed us to complete the deliverance. Trust me, God has given us authority over demons, however decree-and-declare has gone to the other extreme. Decree-and-declare attributes too much authority to believers.

God has not given us all authority

> *And Jesus came and spoke to them, saying, "All authority has been given to <u>Me</u> in heaven and on earth" … (Matthew 28:18, emphasis mine)*

All authority has been given to Jesus. He alone has all authority. Nowhere did it say He gave <u>us</u> all authority. He gave us <u>some</u> authority – only to do what He called us to do.

People often say that every miracle Jesus did, the apostles also did. But that is not true. The apostles healed the sick and cast out demons, which of course Jesus authorized them to do. But there are many miracles that Jesus did that were never emulated. Jesus walked on water. He calmed a storm. He commanded the winds and waves to cease. No one in the Bible emulated that. Paul was in numerous shipwrecks, but he never calmed a storm. Why is that? Because Jesus never gave him authority to do that. Jesus twice multiplied loaves and fishes, and once turned water into wine; yet none of His disciples ever emulated that. If Jesus has given us authority to multiply food, then why don't we all just open restaurants?

I have heard preachers use the following scripture to prove that Christians have authority to call forth things that do not exist into existence.

> *… (as it is written, "I have made you a father of many nations") in the presence of Him whom he believed—<u>God, who</u> gives life to the dead and calls those things which do not exist as though they did … (Romans 4:17, emphasis mine)*

All I can do in response to this is shake my head and laugh. Doesn't this scripture state clearly and unmistakably that it is God who has the authority to *"call those things which are not as if they were"*? Or am I missing something? If we had that authority, why would we even need to depend on God at all?

Well aren't we supposed to be like God? In some ways yes, and in some ways no. The communicable attributes of God are those characteristics that He calls us to emulate. For example, God is love, and we are called to love others. We are called to be holy as God is holy. The incommunicable attributes of God are those we cannot emulate. God is omnipotent – all powerful. He is omnipresent – everywhere at the same time. He is sovereign. The authority and power described in Romans 4 refer to an incommunicable attribute of God that is inextricably linked to His sovereignty.

The most fundamental flaw of decree-and-declare is that it assigns to the believer authority that God has never given us. It attributes too much authority to us. It takes emphasis totally away from God and places it on us. It does not display any dependence on God, which is what faith is. I would not even be going too far if I said that decree-and-declare is anti-faith.

In the next chapter we will look at the various scriptures that are used to propagate this myth of decree-and-declare, and we will learn the right way to make declarations in our prayer.

CHAPTER 2

WHAT THE BIBLE SAYS ABOUT DECREE-AND-DECLARE

In the last chapter, we learned that decree-and-declare overestimates the authority that Jesus has given us, and causes us to speak to circumstances rather than pray to God. This chapter looks at the specific scriptures that speak about decree-and-declare.

Whenever I tell people decree-and-declare is unscriptural, they go immediately to Bible Gateway or any place they can find a concordance, and they search the words *"decree"* and *"declare"*. Any scripture that contains those words, they show me. I tell them that because a word is in the Bible does not mean that a concept is scriptural. *Murder* is in the Bible, but we are not called to do that. We have to look at how the word is used.

Decree-and-declare scriptures

There are two scriptures that are especially noteworthy regarding decree-and-declare. The first one is Job 22:28.

Thou shalt also decree a thing, and it shall be established unto thee ... (Job 22:28, KJV)

People show me this scripture with a smug look on their face, happy to build an entire doctrine on this one verse. They remind me of a skit on Sesame Street where an elephant was lost and looking for the zoo. So he politely enquired of a bystander, *"Excuse me, could you tell me where the zoo is?"* The bystander was eager to help. *"Sure no problem, just go...",* *"OK thank you"*, the elephant interrupted, and he went. A couple of minutes later, he returned, *"Go where?"*

Don't be like that elephant. Don't jump to conclusions based on incomplete information. Don't jump to a conclusion based on parts of the scripture. Read the whole scripture and then form a conclusion.

Job 22:28 clearly says we can decree a thing and it shall be established. Here is an important question to ask when you read anything in the Bible – <u>who said it</u>? The authors of the Bible wrote under the inspiration of the Holy Spirit. So if God said something, or if the author of a Bible book said something, we need to take heed. But very often, the authors quoted other people who may or may not be right.

For example, the psalmist tells us that the fool believes there is no God *(Psalm 14:1)*. The fool is obviously wrong. But the psalmist is correct when he records what the fool incorrectly believes. It does not mean what the fool believes is right. Look at another example. A blind man said that God does not hear sinners *(John 9:31)*. Again, John merely recorded what this man said, but what this man said is questionable at best. If God does not hear sinners, how did you get saved? The Bible records stuff that people said and believed that may or may not be true. This does not mean the Bible is wrong.

Now back to Job 22:28. If God had said we can decree, that would settle it. I would have no need to write this chapter. If Job had said it, it might also have had some credence. But it was actually one of Job's friends called Eliphaz, the Temanite who said these words. The next question to ask is <u>how reliable was Eliphaz</u>? Was Eliphaz right, or was this another example of the Bible recording the words of a misguided soul? Would you believe that the Bible actually answers this question for us? We don't have to speculate.

> *...the Lord said to Eliphaz the Temanite, "My wrath is aroused against you and your two friends, for you have not spoken of Me what is right, as My servant Job has" ... (Job 42:7)*

In this verse, we see God rebuking Eliphaz and his friends for not speaking that which was right. Does this mean everything Eliphaz said is wrong? No. But it certainly means he is not credible. In stark contrast to the authors of scriptures who were inspired by God, here is God openly and emphatically discrediting Eliphaz for talking trash. And you let this guy teach you how to pray? You make this guy the leading scriptural authority on decree-and-declare? Job 22:28 simply records that Eliphaz said we could decree. But Eliphaz was wrong. Don't be like Eliphaz.

Declare God's decrees

Another scripture with the words decree and declare is Psalm 2:7,

> *I will declare the decree: The Lord has said to Me, 'You are My Son, Today I have begotten You'*

This verse actually contains both words. But it does not quite come across as *"decree and declare"*, does it? It's more like *"declare the decree"*. Look at the structure of that verse. The decree is the part that comes after the colon – *"the Lord has said ..."* The decree is what God said. The psalmist is vowing to declare God's decree.

This verse stands in complete contrast to the *"decree-and-declare"* movement, which claims that God has given us authority to decree. Far from it! God is the one who decrees. We can declare His decrees. Scriptural declarations are based on what God has decreed, not what we decree or what we want.

Decree is a legislative term that means to enact something into law. For example, we see earthly kings making decrees or laws. Their decrees became law and they were enforced.

> *If it pleases the king, let a royal <u>decree</u> go out from him, and let it be recorded in the laws of the Persians and the Medes, so that <u>it will not be altered</u> ... (Esther 1:19, emphasis mine)*

> *Now, O king, <u>establish the decree</u> and <u>sign the writing</u>, so that it <u>cannot be changed</u>, according to the law of the Medes and Persians ... (Daniel 6:8, emphasis mine)*

Do you think the same thing happens when you decree? Really? In the spiritual realm, God has reserved that right for Himself. He makes decrees that cannot pass away. There is no place in scripture where God has passed on that right to us. God did not resign from His job. Why do we even see the need to decree? God's decrees are perfect. His Word is forever settled in heaven. We cannot improve on God's decrees.

Our job is to declare God's decrees. A police officer can enforce laws, but has no authority to enact laws. Only the legislative arm of the government can do that. Similarly, we cannot decree spiritual things. We can declare what God has decreed.

When Job got sick and his wife told him to curse God and die, Job responded

> *"Naked came I out of my mother's womb, and naked shall I return thither: the Lord gave, and the Lord hath taken away; blessed be the name of the Lord." ... Though he slay me, yet will I trust in him ... For I know that my redeemer liveth, and that he shall stand at the latter day upon the earth ... (Job 1:21, 13:15, 19:25, KJV)*

Job was declaring the sovereignty of God and his unwavering commitment to Him regardless of His blessings. He was declaring his complete confidence in God's ability to deliver him either in this life or the next.

When the devil was throwing all his fiery darts against Paul, he wrote

We are hard-pressed on every side, yet not crushed; we are perplexed, but not in despair; persecuted, but not forsaken; struck down, but not destroyed ... (2 Corinthians 4:8-9)

Paul was declaring that no matter what the devil threw at him, the God he served was greater, and not even the devil's best attempts could thwart the purposes of God in their lives.

When you go through trials and you feel the temptation to get angry with God, recognize that it is the devil putting those thoughts in your mind. Declare to him,

"Devil, you are only bringing this trial because God allowed you to do it. You have been defeated and you are powerless to do anything unless God permits it. My God is able to deliver me, and He is able to do exceedingly abundantly above all I can ask or think. In all these things, I am more than a conqueror in Christ. And even if God chooses to not deliver me in this life, in the absolute worst-case scenario, I will be rejoicing with the angels in heaven while you and your minions will be bound hand and foot in the lake of fire. Worst-case scenario devil, I win and you lose."

When you are discouraged about your unsaved loved ones, declare out loud,

"Devil, I know the Word says that you have blinded the minds of the unbelieving, but the Word also says that the gospel is the power of God unto salvation. Jesus in me is greater than the devil who is in the world. If God could save the apostle Paul, He could save my unsaved loved ones."

"Lord I pray for your conviction upon their lives, and that You will remove the scales from their eyes like You did with the apostle Paul. Open their eyes Lord, and draw them to you."

This way you use the Word of God as a sword in the devil's heart. Isn't this so much better than these vain repetitions? Isn't this so much better than *"speaking into their lives"*?

Pray how Jesus taught us to pray

Jesus is infinitely wise. He knew that one day, the devil would send his seducing spirits to pervert the way Christians pray. So He took the initiative to teach us exactly how to pray. Not only that, He also taught us how <u>not</u> to pray – don't pray to impress others, don't make vain repetitions.

> *And when you pray, <u>you shall not be like the hypocrites</u>. For they love to pray standing in the synagogues and on the corners of the streets, <u>that they may be seen by men</u>. Assuredly, I say to you, they have their reward. But you, when you pray, go into your room, and when you have shut your door, <u>pray to your Father</u> who is in the secret place; and your Father who sees in secret will <u>reward you openly</u>. And when you pray, <u>do not use vain repetitions</u> as the heathen do. For they think that they will be heard for their many words ... (Matthew 6:5-7, emphasis mine)*

The Lord's Prayer is a humble petition that recognizes the authority of God, and trusts Him to answer us. Decree-and-declarists trust in their own self-appointed authority. God resists the proud, and exalts the humble. Pray the way Jesus taught us to pray. Reject these new teachings. Decree-and-declare is not a measure of spiritual maturity and stature. It is a measure of your gullibility and lack of grounding in the Word of God. Reject these vain babblings. Don't make God resist your prayers because of pride. Humble yourself before Him and <u>ask</u> Him for what you need.

MYTH #2

THE DEVIL IS HINDERING MY PRAYERS

How this myth keeps us in bondage

This is a myth that makes the devil big and God small. It believes that we must do something about the devil before we can receive God's blessings. This myth is a decoy of the devil to distract us into the wrong warfare. As a result our prayers are misguided and ineffective.

What you will learn in the next two chapters

- The devil cannot steal from us or from God
- God is in control
- Spiritual warfare is not about taking back anything from the devil
- We are not under generational curses, but a generational blessing
- We should instead search ourselves for hindrances to prayer
- We should rest in God's sovereignty when we don't get our way

Let the truth free you from the burden of believing you have to fight the devil for God to hear and answer your prayer. Let the truth free you from the burden of believing that the devil has stolen your blessings and you must find a way to take them back. Let the truth free you from the burden of believing you are walking under generational curses that you must break before you see God's blessings in your life.

CHAPTER 3

DO WE HAVE TO TAKE BACK WHAT THE DEVIL STOLE?

Sometime ago, I was listening to a well-known TV preacher who explained how the spiritual realm works.

"We wrestle against spiritual wickedness in high places. But Jesus is seated in heavenly places, which is above the high places. We are on earth, Satan is in the high places, and Jesus is in the heavenly places.

Therefore when we pray, our prayers have to go through the high places which are controlled by Satan before they reach to Jesus. So if there is any flaw in our prayers, Satan gives it a thumbs-down and God cannot answer it.

Also when God does answer our prayers, the answer must pass back through the high places (Satan's domain) to get to us. So very often, Satan steals the answer to our prayer.

Therefore it is our job to pray proper prayers, and to go after the devil and take back what he stole, take back the answers to our prayers." [3]

I skipped two lines, because it takes a while to inhale all that garbage. How small is your god? And how big is your devil? If God is that small, we are better off serving Judge Judy. When she makes a ruling, it is final. This theology acts as though the devil is a big bad bully who shoves God around and takes away His lunch money. It acts as though God is hand-cuffed, blindfolded and gagged, and He is begging us *"please do something about the devil"*. That god is small. That god is not the God of the Bible. This myth makes God small and the devil big.

Here is a variation of this myth. Another person was talking about her prayer life and she narrated the following revelation she received:

"I was praying and pleading the blood of Jesus over all the walls in my house. Then I heard a voice say, "Why are you leaving out the ceiling and the floor?" So I said "Thank you Lord" and I started pleading the blood over all the

walls, the ceiling and floor. And oh heck, let's throw in the windows and the doors as well. The Bible says to give no place for the devil." ⁴

I skipped two more lines. I think she left out the telephone lines and wireless connections. What about the cable? And oh my, I hope she does not have a satellite dish, because then she would have to plead the blood over the entire stratosphere.

It is bondage to think you need to "apply God's protection" over every square inch every minute of every day. The obvious problem with this "revelation" is that it makes the devil bigger than he really is. These teachings turn God's protection into a fragile thing, and causes us to live in constant fear of losing it. You only need to pray for God's protection – plain and simple – *"deliver us from the evil one"* (Matthew 6:13).

Just as an aside, the expression *"plead the blood"*, as popular as it is, does not appear anywhere in the Bible. I really hate to nitpick. If you wish to pray that way, it's fine, it's not really a big deal. The truth is that the blood of Jesus is continually working on your behalf whether or not you plead it. The truth is that Jesus is the one actually pleading the blood on your behalf since He is your advocate *(defense lawyer)*, who is ever making intercession for you.

> *But if we walk in the light as He is in the light, we have fellowship with one another, and the blood of Jesus Christ His Son cleanses us from all sin ... (1 John 1:7)*
>
> *...if anyone sins, we have an Advocate with the Father, Jesus Christ the righteous ... (1 John 2:1)*
>
> *Therefore He is also able to save to the uttermost those who come to God through Him, since He always lives to make intercession for them ... (Hebrews 7:25)*

These myths imply that we need to do something about the devil before we can receive the blessings of God. So instead of praying <u>for</u> God's kingdom, we are constantly praying <u>against</u> the devil's kingdom. Instead of praying to God boldly in confidence, we now have to be careful how we word our prayers, and then we have the added dimension of taking back what the devil stole. It's too much. It is bondage.

These myths change the way we pray and cause us to pray amiss. Our precious prayer time is now spent taking back what the devil supposedly stole. We even sing songs about it, where we go through all the motions of stamping on the devil with our feet, and taking back what he stole. This is a distraction of the enemy.

What Ephesians really says

The preacher above made reference to these verses from the book of Ephesians:

> *He raised Him from the dead and <u>seated Him at His right hand in the heavenly places</u>, far above all principality and power and might and dominion, and every name that is named, not only in this age but also in that which is to come ... (Ephesians 1:20-21, emphasis mine)*

> *For we wrestle not against flesh and blood, but against principalities, against powers, against the rulers of the darkness of this world, against <u>spiritual wickedness in high places</u> ... (Ephesians 6:12, emphasis mine)*

We do wrestle against spiritual wickedness in high places. That is true. Christ is seated in heavenly places above principalities and powers. That is also true. But he missed a crucial verse.

> *But God ... raised us up together, and made us sit together in the heavenly places in Christ Jesus ... (Ephesians 2:4-6)*

That makes a huge difference, doesn't it? If you were not familiar with those verses of scripture, wouldn't you agree that reading them now has a truly liberating effect? The Bible says you shall know the truth and the truth shall set you free.

In complete contrast to that preacher's worldview, Ephesians places us in the heavenly places with Christ. Our prayers don't have to go through the devil to get to God. Our prayers are <u>not</u> subject to veto by the devil. And the answers to our prayers don't get stolen by the devil. When we pray, we operate in a sphere way above the devil's pay grade. The devil does not have the necessary clearance to touch our prayers, as the old hymn says, *"When I kneel in prayer and with Thee my God, I commune as friend with Friend."* [5]

Does Satan have an underwater kingdom?

In recent times there has been a spurt of testimonies by people who claimed they were heavily involved in Satanism, but were delivered and are now serving Jesus. Praise God if that is true. Now that they are saved, they are exposing Satan's secrets so that Christians can wage a proper warfare against the devil. They claim that Satan has a secret underwater kingdom, and that demons are especially active between midnight and 3 am. They suggest that is the time our prayers are most effective.

What do you think? Here are some questions to consider.
1) If they were truly delivered, why are they not forsaking their old teachings, and humbly submitting themselves to learn from the Word of God?
2) Why are they teaching Satanist doctrines in the church? Doctrine comes from the Word of God, not from Satanism.
3) Why does the Bible say nothing about water spirits? In fact, Satan is called the prince of the air (*Ephesians 2:2*), not the prince of the water. The Bible clearly places Satan in the high places.
4) If the Bible did not tell us Satan's precise location, is it really that important for us to know?
5) Why did the Bible say to pray always, rather than to pray between 12 – 3 am?
6) Is it possible that some of these individuals were just planted by the devil to distract the church into a warfare that we are not called to fight?

What the Bible says about spiritual warfare

We used to sing a song in church about going into the enemy's camp and taking back what he stole from us. It was a catchy song and it came with actions and all. It was a feel good song. You could not sing that song and remain sad. But it's based on a misunderstanding of spiritual warfare. The songwriter most likely was referring to David when the Amalekites had stolen all his possession. David encouraged himself in the Lord, then went in God's power to fight the enemy and take back what they stole. But this has absolutely nothing to do with New Testament spiritual warfare.

I used to think spiritual warfare was just a spiritual version of Old Testament warfare. In the Old Testament, Israel was commanded to invade and take over the enemy's land. This was their warfare. So I thought, in the New Testament, we do the exact same thing, except that we are not fighting against flesh and blood (*human enemies*), but spiritual enemies. So if Israel invaded and took over their enemies' lands, then we should invade the devil's territory and take over / take back what he stole. Take back our unsaved loved ones' salvation. Take back our prosperity. Take back our healing.

The problem is that when you read the New Testament scriptures on spiritual warfare, these ideas simply do not come across. For example, look at Ephesians 6.

Finally, my brethren, be strong in the Lord and in the power of His might. Put on the whole armor of God, <u>that you may be able to stand against the wiles of</u>

the devil. For we do not wrestle against flesh and blood, but against principalities, against powers, against the rulers of the darkness of this age, against spiritual hosts of wickedness in the heavenly places. Therefore take up the whole armor of God, <u>that you may be able to withstand in the evil day</u>, and having done all, to stand.

Stand therefore, having girded your waist with truth, having put on the breastplate of righteousness, and having shod your feet with the preparation of the gospel of peace; above all, taking the shield of faith with which you will be able to quench all the <u>fiery darts of the wicked one</u>. And take the helmet of salvation, and the sword of the Spirit, which is the word of God

… Ephesians 6:10-17, emphasis mine

For the time being, focus only on the big picture. What is the image of warfare that is being painted by the Apostle Paul? Pretend that there is a play button which shows you a video version of the scripture, seeing that the language is so graphic. What is the movie that plays in the background as you read those words? Does it look like a spiritual version of *Rambo* where Christians go into the enemy's territory, armed with Holy Ghost machine guns, sending demons scattering in all directions? Does it paint a picture of Christians going into hospitals and putting doctors out of business? The answer is a resounding no. It does not.

It paints a picture of the devil coming against us, and of us defending ourselves. It talks about an evil day when we have to fight against the evil one, and having done all, to stand. It sounds brutal. To help us in this battle, we are given an armor consisting of six elements – the helmet of salvation, the breastplate of righteousness, the girdle belt of truth, shoes representing the gospel of peace, the shield of faith, and the sword of the Spirit – the Word of God.

Five of the 6 elements are clearly defensive in nature, and the sword can be used defensively and offensively. So I would say the armor is 90% defensive. Also pay attention to what our weapons are – being saved, living righteously, living in truth, preaching the gospel i.e. effective Christian living – not taking back what the devil stole.

Paul was in a Roman jail when he wrote the book of Ephesians. He was most likely inspired to write these words when he saw the Roman soldiers garbed in their military armor. But the Holy Spirit only inspired Paul to list six parts of the armor. There were other offensive components of the Roman armor that Paul left out. I am sure you have seen movies like *Gladiator*. They had a long jousting spear *(called a lance)* that they used to knock opponents off their horses. They had a spiky metal ball *(called a flail or a mace)*. They also had arrows that were used for long distance combat. All of these offensive weapons were deliberately left out of the Christian armor. In fact in Ephesians 6, the devil is the one with fiery arrows, not us.

The Holy Spirit was making it clear that Christian warfare is not as offensive as we would like to think. Yes I know that as Charismatic Christians, we love the idea of scattering demons wherever we go. This is simply not the picture of warfare that is being painted.

Having said that, there is something very powerful about being able to walk through the valley of the shadow of death knowing we are protected in Christ, even if we are not the aggressors in the spiritual battle. There is something powerful about doing God's work knowing that demons are powerless to harm us unless God allows them.

In the Old Testament, Israel was given an invade-and-take-over mandate. In the New Testament, Christians are given more of a spy-infiltration type warfare.

Would you like to be a spy?

Once while I was studying in the US, a CIA representative visited our society to recruit spies. He gave a brief talk, then asked for volunteers. Some people raised their hands. Admittedly, those were the people who looked like what the CIA might hire. But he seemed uninterested in them. He then walked over to me, put his hand on my shoulder, and asked if I was interested in being a spy with the CIA. I just smiled to myself because it was painfully obvious that he was looking for the guy who looked the least like James Bond. At that moment, I finally realized I was old.

Being a spy is not as exciting as you think. The job often consists of laborious work and most of the time is spent in boring debriefing sessions. Similarly, New Testament warfare is not a spiritual version of *Rambo*. The imagery painted by the Apostle Paul is one of spies going into enemy territory, not to take over the land, but with the goal of rescuing as many hostages as we could in the short time that we have. In the process, the enemy's intelligence agencies have detected our activity, and he has unleashed his forces against us to hinder us. But spiritually we are in an armored tank *(more on this in later chapters)*. In the midst of trials, we are to resist the devil and persevere with our mission. This is precisely what Paul told Timothy:

> *You therefore must endure hardship as a good soldier of Jesus Christ. No one engaged in warfare entangles himself with the affairs of this life, that he may please him who enlisted him as a soldier … (2 Timothy 2:3-4)*

Jesus Himself endured all the devil threw at Him and remained steadfast in His mission. He is our example.

> *... Jesus, the author and finisher of our faith, who for the joy that was set before Him endured the cross, despising the shame, and has sat down at the right hand of the throne of God ... (Hebrews 12:2)*

<u>That is New Testament warfare – living right and resisting the devil as we do God's work.</u> Did I miss the part where we take back what the enemy stole? That's because it's not there.

But didn't the devil hinder Daniel's prayers?

> *<u>At the beginning of your supplications</u> the command went out, and I have come to tell you, for you are greatly beloved; therefore consider the matter, and understand the vision ... (Daniel 9:23, emphasis mine)*

> *Then he said to me, "Do not fear, Daniel, for <u>from the first day</u> that you set your heart to understand, and to humble yourself before your God, your words were heard; and I have come because of your words. But the <u>prince of the kingdom of Persia withstood me twenty-one days</u>; and behold, Michael, one of the chief princes, came to help me, for I had been left alone there with the kings of Persia ... (Daniel 10:12-13, emphasis mine)*

These are two occasions when Daniel prayed and God sent an angel to answer him. On both occasions, the angel told Daniel that God heard him the first day he started to pray. However, on the second occasion, the angel took 3 weeks to get to Daniel with the answer because the devil's forces had hindered him.

Hmmm, this sure looks like the devil hindered the answer to Daniel's prayer. Yes, but where did it say the devil stole anything? Where did it say that Daniel had to go and take back anything from the devil? All Daniel did was pray and fast. That is the lesson we should take away. Keep praying and fasting. Of course the devil could hinder us. He hindered Paul.

> *...we wanted to come to you ... but Satan hindered us ... (1 Thess. 2:18)*

Paul did not seem to think that any serious warfare was needed. He did not bind or rebuke the devil. He did not exclaim, "THE DEVIL IS A LIAR!" He simply said, *"Satan hindered us, whatever."* He actually seemed to imply that Satan hindering him was God's way of directing his paths, i.e. God used Satan to direct Paul's path.

On another occasion, God led Paul by giving him a vision of a man inviting him to preach (*Acts 16:9-10*). So these are two occasions when Paul wanted to go one place, but ended up going somewhere else. In the second instance, it was God who directed Paul. In the first instance, it was Satan who hindered Paul. The end result is that Paul went somewhere preaching the gospel. He did not seem overly alarmed. He acted as though God allowed Satan to hinder him because God had other plans. Did you get that? He acted as though God is big and the devil is small. He acted as though God is in control. Paul simply prayed for God to open doors, and he acknowledged that God could direct his paths in numerous ways. Sometimes He used dreams and visions, sometimes He used providence and circumstance, and sometimes He used the devil. But every time, God was in the driver's seat. God is big. The devil is small.

Here are some lessons we can learn from Daniel.
1) God hears us from the moment we start to pray. In fact God knows what you need before you even pray.
2) Sometimes He answers right away, sometimes He delays.
3) The devil may hinder the answers to our prayers if God allows it.
4) If God wants us to have something, He will ensure that we get it.
5) Sometimes we need to add fasting to our prayer.

Don't let the devil distract you

Magicians work by distraction. They direct your attention in one place, while they perform a sleight of hand trick where you are not looking. That's how they baffle you. If you think about it, these myths are a very clever distraction strategy of the devil. This is how he baffles Christians and keeps us in bondage. Distraction is one of the major strategies of the devil in his war against us. He wants us to get sidetracked into a fistfight with Him. Every minute we waste taking back what the devil stole is a minute that we don't spend praying for unsaved people or sharing the gospel with them.

If the devil hinders, it is only because God allows it. (*We will talk much more about this in later chapters.*) Daniel just kept praying and fasting and humbling himself before God. Daniel did not change his modus operandi simply because he wasn't getting his prayer answered in his timing. Sometimes you just have to be consistent at doing the right things.

In the next chapter, we will look at another myth that is very similar to this one, and dear to many people's heart – is there a generational curse that is responsible for me not getting my prayers answered, for the circumstances in my life, or even for the choices I have made?

CHAPTER 4

AM I UNDER A GENERATIONAL CURSE?

Have you ever gone through a trial, and realized that everyone in your family has gone through the same thing? Perhaps you noticed that members of your family take long to get married or never marry. Or every one of your brothers and sisters ended up getting divorced. Maybe you know another family where everyone dies young or gets killed in an untimely fashion. Then you wonder if there is some kind of generational curse that needs to be broken.

The belief that Christians can be under a generational curse is similar to what we discussed in the last chapter. It is a variation of the belief that we must do something about the devil in order to release the blessings of God. In this case, God wants to bless us, but the devil has cursed us – so too bad for God. He wants to bless us, but He can't. But if we can break the curse, then God's blessings will flow. It is not hard to see how this myth makes the devil big and God small. <u>This is a myth that believes that God cannot bless what the devil has cursed</u>. There are so many things wrong with that belief.

1) The Bible says the exact opposite – what God blesses, no one can curse (*Numbers 23:8*).
2) The devil has no power or authority to curse anything or anyone.

The reason Christians believe they are under a generational curse is because they believe that the devil truly has independent power to hinder our prayers and to control our lives. We first of all assume that there is a curse. Secondly we assume that the devil is the one responsible for this curse. Finally we must break the curse. Essentially we have to do something about the devil before we can enjoy the blessings of God.

Generational curses often become a self-fulfilling prophecy. For example, if someone believes they are under a curse of divorce, they may end up getting divorced because they throw in the towel at the first hurdle in their marriage thinking that they cannot fight the inevitable. They then conclude that they got divorced because of a generational curse.

What the Bible says about generational curses

> *For I, the Lord your God, am a jealous God, visiting the iniquity of the fathers upon the children to the third and fourth generations of those who hate Me, but showing mercy to thousands, to those who love Me and keep My commandments ... (Exodus 20:4-6, emphasis mine)*

Immediately you should notice three things about that scripture.
1) God is the one who brings generational curses. He is the one who visits the iniquity of the parents to the 3rd and 4th generation. It is not the devil who is responsible for generational curses. It is God.
2) God curses those who hate Him (*not those who love Him*).
3) God blesses those who love Him to 1000 generations.

A good example of a family that was cursed by God was Eli, the priest. Eli's sons were wicked and Eli was negligent. As a result, God pronounced that every male in Eli's lineage would die young (*1 Samuel 2:31-33*). Now if I were one of Eli's grandsons, I would find that really unfair. I did nothing wrong and now I am under a curse. And you may be wondering if you are in a similar situation. Did your parents or grandparents do or say anything that placed you under a curse? It is a very fair question.

Since it is God who pronounces generational curses, binding the devil and trying to break the curse is pointless. You cannot rebuke, bind or break God. Here is something else to think about. God's generational curses last 3 or 4 generations, while His blessings on those who love Him extend to a thousand generations. I don't even think there has been a thousand generations in recorded human history.

Why is it that we assume we are under a curse rather than a blessing? Is it because we are not getting everything we want? Is it because we are so preoccupied by what we do not have, and we forget all the good things that God has given us? Is it because we think the devil's curses are stronger than God's blessings?

Suppose your grandfather consulted a voodoo priest and invoked a generational curse from God. But suppose your great-great-great grandfather was a pastor who inherited a generational blessing. The generational curse is unto the 3rd and 4th generation, but the generational blessing is unto 1000 generations. Which one do you fall under? What if no one in your genealogy was righteous, but you are born-again, then shouldn't a brand new generational blessing start with you?

Look at what else the Bible says about generational curses.

> *'What do you mean when you use this proverb concerning the land of Israel, saying: 'The fathers have eaten sour grapes, and the children's teeth are set on*

> edge'? "As I live" says the Lord God, "you shall no longer use this proverb in Israel" ... (Ezekiel 18:2-3)
>
> *But every one shall die for his own iniquity; every man who eats the sour grapes, his teeth shall be set on edge ... (Jeremiah 31:30)*

The people were saying *"it makes no sense living righteously because my fathers sinned and I am under a generational curse"*. So if they were cursed, what was the point? But God refuted that line of reasoning. He said everyone is responsible for their own sin. Essentially God is saying that whatever your ancestors may have done, and whether or not that invoked a generational curse, you can change it.

Daniel was blessed while under a curse

If anyone was under a generational curse, it was Daniel. His ancestors had sinned and rebelled against God for hundreds of years. They worshipped Baal and Ashtoreth, and they passed their children over fire. Anything that is blasphemous, idolatrous, and profane, they did it. So God allowed Nebuchadnezzar to take them captive in Babylon for 70 years. Daniel was a young man when this happened. He did nothing wrong, but he found himself in captivity because of what his ancestors had done.

But Daniel was a righteous man who sought the Lord. Because of this, God blessed him and promoted him to be the ruler over the entire province of Babylon. Even though his nation remained in captivity, Daniel was able to rise above that because of God's favor.

The same thing is true of us. In the midst of a crooked and perverse generation, we shine as lights *(Philippians 2:15)*. When all of nature around us is wallowing under a curse, we are more than conquerors through Christ *(Romans 8:27)*. As a child of God, Jesus has set you free. He became a curse that the blessings of Abraham would come on us.

> *Christ has redeemed us from the curse of the law, having become a curse for us (for it is written, "Cursed is everyone who hangs on a tree"), that the blessing of Abraham might come upon the Gentiles in Christ Jesus, that we might receive the promise of the Spirit through faith ... (Galatians 3:13-14)*

Regardless of what our ancestors did, our spiritual father Abraham was righteous and he pleased God. Even better, Jesus is our righteousness and He became the curse for us. We are not under any generational curse, but rather the blessings of Abraham.

But because God is not giving us all we want, we look for formulas that allow us to get our prayers answered without having to actually trust God. We look for answers to prayer and blessings without any regard for righteousness. There may be reasons other than generational curses why your prayers are not being answered. We should search ourselves to see if there are any hindrances to our prayers.

Hindrances to prayer

Sometimes the reason God does not answer or delays His answer is due to our negligence. Sometimes it is because of His will and His timing. We cannot always know for sure, but we should ensure that there are no hindrances to prayer in our lives. Sometimes God will choose to not bless us until we deal with these hindrances. Here are some possible hindrances to prayer.

Not praying

You lust and do not have. You murder and covet and cannot obtain. You fight and war. Yet you do not have because you do not ask ... (James 4:2)

Praying amiss or selfishly

You ask and do not receive, because you ask amiss, that you may spend it on your pleasures ... (James 4:3)

Not praying according to God's will

Now this is the confidence that we have in Him, that if we ask anything according to His will, He hears us ... (1 John 5:14)

Harboring unforgiveness

... if you do not forgive men their trespasses, neither will your Father forgive your trespasses ... (Matthew 6:15)

Having family relationship problems

Husbands, likewise, dwell with them with understanding, giving honor to the wife, as to the weaker vessel, and as being heirs together of the grace of life, that your prayers may not be hindered ... (1 Peter 3:7)

Pride

God resists the proud, but gives grace to the humble ... (James 4:6)

Being double minded or unstable in your walk with God

But let him ask in faith, with no doubting, for he who doubts is like a wave of the sea driven and tossed by the wind. For let not that man suppose that he will receive anything from the Lord; he is a double-minded man, unstable in all his ways ... (James 1:6-8)

Sin

Behold, the Lord's hand is not shortened that it cannot save; nor His ear heavy, that it cannot hear. But your iniquities have separated you from your God; and your sins have hidden His face from you, So that He will not hear ... (Isaiah 59:1-2)

Recognize that God is sovereign

Sometimes we have to simply accept that something may not be God's will or God's timing. Sad to say, sometimes we may not receive the blessing in our lifetime.

These all died in faith, <u>not</u> having received the promises, but having seen them afar off were assured of them, embraced them and confessed that they were strangers and pilgrims on the earth ... (Hebrews 11:13, emphasis mine)

Revelation 5:8 further tells us that the prayers of the saints are stored in vials to be opened in God's timing. The martyrs who were slain for the Word of God were crying out to God, *"How long, O Lord?" (Revelation 6:10)*. These martyrs had died yet their prayers remained unanswered. It is a fact that God is not going to grant all your requests – get over it. But notice that the martyrs still prayed <u>to God</u>. They did not change the way they prayed simply because God was not answering. They did not embrace new strategies to get their prayers answered and to move the hand of God. And the Bible never condemned them for it. For whatever reason, God's will and timing are often different from ours, and we just have to accept that.

The prosperity gospel has spoiled us into setting our affections on earthly things. It has conditioned us to associate material blessings with God's favor. But the Bible teaches that we should not set our affections on things of the earth, and that godliness with contentment is great gain.

Don't change the way you pray to keep up with the times. God has not changed. You don't have to pray against the devil, just pray to God. Not getting answers is not a reason for changing the way you pray. Be consistent at doing what the Bible says. Keep praying, fasting, and seeking Him, and remember it is better sometimes to just let God be God.

MYTH #3

I NEED TO BIND THE DEVIL'S KINGDOM

How this myth keeps us in bondage

This is a myth that makes the devil big and God small. We act as though God can't do anything about the devil so we must step up to the plate. We end up spending most of our time praying <u>against</u> the devil rather than praying <u>to</u> God. As a result our prayers miss their mark and become ineffective.

What you will learn in the next two chapters

- What the Bible actually says about binding and loosing
- Binding and loosing is about church discipline and church governance, not prayer and warfare
- Jesus already bound the strongman, so all we need to do is plunder the devil's house
- When to petition God, and when to command the devil

Let the truth free you from the burden of believing that until you bind the devil you cannot walk in God's blessings. Let the truth free you from the burden of having to identify and bind the strongman in every single situation you face for the rest of your life.

CHAPTER 5

THE TRUE MEANING OF BINDING AND LOOSING

Are your prayers missing their target?

In the movie *Dumb and Dumber*, there is a scene at the end where Jeff Daniels' character Harry *(the one who is not Jim Carrey)* bursts into a hotel room where his best friend and his love-interest are being held captive by the bad guy. But unbeknownst to everyone, Harry has a secret weapon – a gun hidden behind his back. At the opportune moment, he pulls out this gun and unloads six bullets in the direction of the bad guy. It was the stuff legends are made of. Harry came close to writing his name in crime-fighting folklore. There was just one problem. Harry was a lousy shot. Every single bullet missed its target. He hit the wall, the lights, the furniture. He completely missed the bad guy six out of six times. Then he ended up getting captured as well. The movie was hilarious, but the fact that this happens to Christians all the time is sad.

Do you feel your prayers are like Harry's bullets – missing everything? Do you feel as though you're firing heavy artillery at the devil, yet your prayers seem to have little to no effect? Well that's exactly what happened to the nation of Israel in 1 Samuel chapter 4. They were in a battle against the Philistines in the days when Eli was high priest. In fact, this was Eli's last day as high priest, because he would lose his life at the end of this battle.

The Philistines had just killed 4,000 of Israel's soldiers, and Israel was in retreat. So the elders called for the Ark of the Covenant. Surely God Himself with them on the battle-field would guarantee victory. When the Israelites saw the Ark, they shouted with such a loud voice, that the Bible says the earth shook. The Philistines heard it *(and I guess they felt it as well)*, and they were scared out of their minds, but they encouraged themselves to fight anyway.

> *God has come into the camp! Woe to us! Who will deliver us from the hand of these mighty gods? These are the gods who struck the Egyptians with all the plagues in the wilderness. ... Be strong and conduct yourselves like men, you*

Philistines, that you do not become servants of the Hebrews, as they have been to you. Conduct yourselves like men, and fight! ... (1 Samuel 4:7-9)

What no one had realized was that the glory of God had departed from Israel. The Philistines defeated them that day, and confiscated the Ark of the Covenant. You can read the entire account in 1 Samuel 4 – it is one of the saddest chapters in the entire Bible.

There are some key lessons to take away from this story:
1) Shouting does not guarantee victory.
2) Yesterday's forms and rituals mean nothing today if God is not in it.
3) Scaring the enemy is not the same as defeating the enemy.

Christians experience a spiritual version of this story all the time. We are in our prayer meetings shouting, binding, loosing, calling down fire from heaven, trampling on the devil. But what do we really accomplish? We are shooting and missing. You could call it praying amiss. We are dancing in circles, and I am sure the demons are there dancing in wider circles around us. We are rolling on the floor under the *"anointing"* and laughing in the *"Spirit"*, and I am sure the demons are there rolling on the floor laughing at us because of how deceived and misguided we are. The high-tech demons are probably messaging each other, *"LOL ROFL TCASDIBMM"*. The last one stands for *"These Christians are so deceived it blows my mind."*

This is what happens in some of our prayer meetings. This is a spiritual reconstruction of 1 Samuel 4. It would be funny if it weren't so true.

CHRISTIAN: I bind you spirit of cancer in Jesus' name. I loose angels against you. I loose God's healing power.

DEMON #1 (patting down himself and looking confused): What just happened? Were you hit?

DEMON #2: No I wasn't. I don't know what is happening, I'm confused. I'm a little scared to be honest.

DEMON #1: I'm scared too, but we're obviously not defeated. Let's keep attacking them.

DEMON #2: BTW who is 'spirit of cancer'?

DEMON #1: IDK. Never heard of him. I always thought cancer was a degenerative disease. Go figure.

CHRISTIAN: Thank you Lord for the victory. [As he leaves the church thinking he really accomplished something].

Does saying "I bind the devil" really bind the devil?

When did binding and loosing become such a staple in our prayer lives? There is not a single person in scripture who used the words *"I bind the devil"* in prayer. Yet there are some people who spend most of their prayer time binding the devil, and perhaps 10% actually communing with God. That doesn't sound right to me.

I heard a deliverance minister narrate the following incident that happened to him. His kids were acting up and he declared out loud *"I bind you devil and I command you to stop in Jesus' name!"* Then the devil spoke these words to him,

How dare you speak to me like that? Don't ever do that again. If you want to preach the gospel, I'll let you preach the gospel. If you want to feed the hungry, I'll permit it. If you want to be a missionary anywhere in the world, I'll allow it. But that thing you just did – don't you ever do that again. [6]

This is how he knew he really got the devil mad, and of course it confirmed that binding the devil was actually working.

There are a number of problems with this story. The most obvious one is that doctrine does not come from what the devil says. There is a tendency among deliverance ministers to derive their understanding of the spirit world from stuff that demons tell them during deliverance sessions. They are not even supposed to be conversing with demons. How do they know those demons are not lying? After all, the devil is the father of lies. They are literally preaching doctrines taught by demons *(1 Timothy 4:1)*.

The devil went on to say that he would permit the preaching of the gospel, but he did not appreciate the binding of his kingdom. Who gave the devil authority to permit anything? Big devil, small god alert! He is acting as though the devil is some big authority figure. Didn't it occur to him that the devil was just throwing a red herring? I am more tempted to do the opposite of what the devil says. I would preach the gospel, and forget the binding thing. After all, preaching the gospel was kind of a big deal to Jesus. I will actually show you that preaching the gospel is the true way to *"bind"* the devil.

The last thing about that story is the minister's certainty that it was really the devil speaking to him. Most likely this was a thought that entered his mind that he attributed to the devil. Of course the devil can plant thoughts in our mind. No one is disputing that. But thoughts can enter our mind from three sources – 1) God, 2) the devil, 3) our flesh.

Jesus said that His sheep know His voice, but oftentimes people say *"God said …"* when it is really their own thoughts and ideas that they are attributing to God. In this case, I am confident that this guy already had these ideas of binding and loosing established in his mind, and he merely imagined that the devil told him what he already believed. It is a classic case of confirmation bias.

What the Bible actually says about binding and loosing

And I will give you the keys of the kingdom of heaven, and whatever you bind on earth will be bound in heaven, and whatever you loose on earth will be loosed in heaven ... (Matthew 16:19)

Assuredly, I say to you, whatever you bind on earth will be bound in heaven, and whatever you loose on earth will be loosed in heaven ... (Matthew 18:18)

These verses clearly teach that we can bind and loose. But <u>what</u> do we bind and loose, <u>how</u> do we do it, and <u>what</u> does it mean? The typical interpretation is that we can bind the devil or his works. The loosing part is more sketchy. Some people say we can loose the blessings of heaven, others say we can loose the angels of God. In the example earlier, the Christian was *"loosing the healing power of God"*. Don't you find it presumptuous to think a human can loose the power of God? Even the most anointed man of God does not have control over the power of God. God gives gifts *"as He wills"* (*1 Corinthians 12:11*).

Typically we adopt a spiritual understanding of the terms *"bind and loose"*. What if I can show you that those terms do not mean what you think they mean? Would it matter, or would you just bind and loose anyway? *"Stop confusing me with facts!"* *"I bind your book in Jesus' name!"*

There are a number of things that are noteworthy about these verses of scripture. The first is that it is exactly the same expression being repeated by Jesus on two separate occasions. The second is that Matthew is the only gospel writer to record those words. This of course does not mean there is anything wrong with it, but it gives us a clue how to interpret it. Matthew originally wrote to a Jewish audience. As a general rule, if you find something in the book of Matthew that you can't find in Mark, Luke and John, chances are that it is Jewish in origin. So binding and loosing may pertain to some Jewish tradition.

Matthew 16 does not have a clear context, so it is subject to a whole wide range of interpretations. Jesus gave Peter the keys of the kingdom and the authority to bind and to loose. Catholics interpret that to mean that the Pope has the authority to amend scripture as he sees fit. Charismatics interpret that to mean that binding and loosing are the keys of the kingdom, and if we want to establish God's kingdom on earth, we must bind the devil's kingdom and loose God's kingdom. Admittedly the logic seems solid, except for the fact that Matthew 18 has a much clearer context. Here is an outline of Matthew 18:

Verses	Topic
1-5	Entering the kingdom as children
6-9	Handling offenses
10-14	God's mercy and forgiveness
15-17	Those who sin against you
18-20	Binding, loosing and agreement
21-35	Parable about forgiveness and mercy

So *"binding and loosing"* is right there in the middle of a discussion on unrepentant people in the church. If someone sins against you, go and tell him his fault. If he does not listen, take two or three witnesses. If he still does not listen, tell the church. If he still does not hear, treat him as an outsider or a heathen. Then Jesus said *"whatever you bind on earth will be bound in heaven, and whatever you loose on earth will be loosed in heaven"*. Contextually, binding and loosing refer to the process of excommunicating someone from the church. It deals with church discipline.

There is an example of it being played out in 1 Corinthians 5. There was someone in the Corinthian church who was having an affair with his step-mother. It had to be Corinth, didn't it? Paul rebuked the Corinthians sharply for not dealing with this. He instructed that they put him out of the church. He used terms like *"delivering him to Satan"* for the *"destruction of the flesh"*. Strong words. If they had continued to allow that individual to fellowship with them, he was more likely to corrupt the other believers than to come to repentance. Paul put it this way – a little leaven leavens the entire lump. This was an example of binding.

Interesting isn't it? We think church is a place for sinners to come and get saved. That is simply not scriptural. We are supposed to preach the gospel and get people saved on the outside, and then bring them to church. Church is a place for Christians to enjoy fellowship.

Now some time between first and second Corinthians, this man was kicked out of the church, and had apparently come to repentance. Then Paul wrote to them a second time asking them to forgive the individual and restore him back into fellowship *(2 Corinthians 2:7-10)*. This is loosing. Notice the parallel between Matthew and Corinthians in the following table.

TOPIC	JESUS	PAUL
Put him out / bind	Matthew 18:17 If he refuses even to hear the church, let him be to you like a heathen	1 Corinthians 5:5,7 Deliver to Satan, purge out the old leaven
Forgive and restore / loose	Matthew 18:15 If he hears you, you have gained your brother.	2 Corinthians 2:7 Forgive and comfort him
Agreement	Matthew 18:18-19 Whatever you bind on earth will be bound in heaven, and whatever you loose on earth will be loosed in heaven. If two of you agree on earth concerning anything that they ask, it will be done for them by My Father in heaven	1 Corinthians 5:4 When you are gathered together, along with my spirit, with the power of our Lord Jesus Christ 2 Corinthians 2:10 Whom you forgive anything, I also forgive

It should be clear from this study that binding and loosing refer to church discipline, and not spiritual warfare. It has nothing to do with prayer. Essentially when you say, *"I bind you devil"*, that's like telling someone *"I veto you in traffic."* Veto has nothing to do with driving. Similarly binding has nothing to do with prayer.

Why Jesus used the words "bind and loose"

So you may ask, why did Jesus use fighting words terms like *"bind and loose"* if He was talking about church discipline? Bind and loose are not really fighting words. You can bind up somebody's wound, and you can loose a knot. There is nothing fighting about those words. It is just that when people say *"I bind you devil"*, they raise their voice on *"bind"* and grind their teeth on the *"nd"*. Sometimes they add a *"huh"* at the end of it. But seriously, I have never heard soldiers in any war movie talk about binding and loosing. I have never heard a gangster threaten to bind a member of an opposing gang. Those are not fighting words. It is just that we Charismatics assign to it a meaning that it does not really have.

So why did Jesus use those words? Why didn't he just say *"Whoever you kick out on earth is kicked out in heaven"*? Good question, I am so glad you asked. It is because Jesus did not speak English. He was using the same language that the Jewish Rabbis used. Remember I mentioned earlier that the binding and loosing scriptures are only found in Matthew, and not the other three gospels. This alludes to Jewish origins.

The Rabbis used the terms bind and loose to refer to obligations they imposed on their followers. The Hillel school of Rabbis tended to be very liberal, while the Shammai school tended to be very strict. The Shammai could bind the people to obey certain laws, but the Hillels might loose them from that obligation.[7]

We see this playing out in Acts 15 when the Jewish Christians were teaching that the Gentiles who converted to Christianity needed to get circumcised in order to be saved (*Acts 15:1*). How did they even know who was circumcised and who was not? The Apostles convened a high-profile meeting, and James spoke to the people.

> *Now therefore, why do you test God by <u>putting a yoke on the neck</u> of the disciples which neither our fathers nor we were able to bear? ... Therefore I judge that <u>we should not trouble those from among the Gentiles</u> who are turning to God ... (Acts 15:10, 19, emphasis mine)*

Their fathers had put a yoke on their neck that they could not carry – they <u>bound</u> them to those laws. James said that they should not attempt to impose those bondages on the Gentiles. So he <u>loosed</u> them from any obligation to Jewish laws. That my friends, is where the terms bind and loose came from, and this is why Jesus used those words. It is a broad set of terms that speak of church discipline and church governance. It does not mean to bind the devil or loose the angels of God. This is another of those myths that make us pray ineffectively.

In the next chapter, we will talk more about binding the strongman and rebuking the devil. We will also investigate what is the correct way to pray according to the Bible. When do we ask God for something? When do we speak to our circumstances?

CHAPTER 6

DO WE HAVE TO BIND THE STRONGMAN?

...how can one enter a strong man's house and plunder his goods, <u>unless he first binds the strong man?</u> And then he will plunder his house ... (Matthew 12:29, emphasis mine)

I deliberately did not address this scripture in the last chapter, because I felt it deserved a chapter on its own. The typical understanding of this verse is that Christians are supposed to bind the strongman. In every situation, we are supposed to identify the strongman – the demon in control – and bind him. Only then can we receive the breakthrough. For example, if you have to preach the gospel in a new place, you have to identify the prevailing spirit over that city, bind him, and then preach the gospel. If you preach the gospel without first binding the strongman, the results will not be as good. But if you bind the strongman first, people will get saved in hordes.

There are a number of flaws with that interpretation. Firstly, no one in the book of Acts ever bound any strongman before they preached the gospel. Secondly, evangelism <u>is</u> warfare. Warfare is not the thing you do before evangelism. The entire process of praying, interceding and preaching – it's all warfare. Ephesians 6:15 tells us that our feet should be shod with the preparation of the gospel of peace. In other words, the gospel itself is a weapon of our warfare. The gospel is the power of God unto salvation.

The last major flaw in that interpretation is that it misunderstands the point Jesus was trying to make in Matthew 12. Jesus was not telling <u>us</u> to bind the strongman, He was telling us that <u>He</u> already bound Satan.

Jesus had just healed a demon-possessed man who was blind and mute. The Pharisees then claimed that He cast out this devil through Beelzebub, the prince of demons. Jesus reasoned with them and showed them logically they were making no sense. Satan does not cast out Satan because Satan's kingdom is not divided against itself. So it was ridiculous for them to conclude that He was casting out Satan with Satan. The only logical alternative was that Jesus was casting out demons by the Spirit of God, and the Kingdom of God had in fact arrived.

Then he continued in verse 29 – *"how can you plunder a strong man's house unless you first bind the strongman?"* Jesus was not telling <u>us</u> to bind the strongman, but rather <u>He</u> already bound the strongman. Look at how Luke narrated the same incident.

> *When a strong man, fully armed, guards his own house, his possessions are undisturbed. But when <u>someone stronger</u> than he attacks him and overpowers him, he takes away from him all his armor on which he had relied and distributes his plunder.... (Luke 11:21-22, NASB, emphasis mine)*

Jesus was the stronger man who bound the strong man, now we can plunder his house. This is why it is even possible to cast out demons. This is why even some of the Pharisees' followers were casting out demons (*Matthew 12:27*). What they were witnessing in Matthew 12 was not the binding of the strongman, but the plundering of his house. We don't have to bind the strongman. Jesus already did that. Our role is to plunder his house.

God binds Satan

It appears that God's kingdom had a binding effect on Satan during Jesus' first coming. Read the Old Testament and you will find only one person who was ever possessed by a demon – that was of course King Saul after God had departed from him. Then we flip over the blank page between Malachi and Matthew, and we find demons everywhere. It appears that during those 400 years of *"silence"* from God, the devil's kingdom grew stronger. Jesus came to a demon possessed world. Even today, demon possession is more common in areas that have not been deeply influenced by the gospel. Somehow God's kingdom and the gospel have a binding effect on the devil. 2 Thessalonians 2:6-7 speak of one who restrains the devil's kingdom. It is God who hinders the devil, not the other way around. Small devil, big God!

Jesus' first coming had a binding effect on Satan. The preaching of the gospel continues to exert a binding effect. After Jesus' second coming, Satan will literally be bound hand and foot in the bottomless pit (*Revelation 20:2*).

In every case, it is God who binds the devil, not us. Our God is big. Don't limit Him by trying to do His job for Him. Don't waste time trying to do what God has already done. We just have to walk in the victory He has already won. We don't have to bind the devil, we just have to plunder the devil's house – preach the gospel, set the captives free, heal the broken hearted, and bind up their wounds.

Binding and rebuking are not the same

I believe that many Christians mistake *"binding"* and *"rebuking"*. They use the terms interchangeably when in fact they do not mean the same thing. Binding means what I have outlined in the last chapter. Rebuking the devil is actually something that is scriptural. Jesus rebuked the devil. Paul rebuked the devil.

> *But Jesus rebuked him, saying, "Be quiet, and come out of him!" … (Mark 1:25)*

> *He rebuked the unclean spirit, saying to it: "Deaf and dumb spirit, I command you, come out of him and enter him no more!" … (Mark 9:25)*

> *But Paul, greatly annoyed, turned and said to the spirit, "I command you in the name of Jesus Christ to come out of her." And he came out that very hour. … (Acts 16:18)*

Rebuking the devil is the same as casting out the devil. If there is a demon at work, then Jesus has given us authority to speak to them and command them to go. Note that they rebuked the demons with the words *"Come out in Jesus' name"*, not *"I rebuke you devil"*.

Saying *"I rebuke you devil"* or *"I bind you devil"* is like a clueless man proposing to his girlfriend. He prepares a candle-light dinner with some soft music in the background to create a romantic mood. Then he takes the diamond ring out of the box, goes down on one knee and whispers the words *"I propose to you in Jesus' name."* Any woman would say to him *"Try again!"* Don't be that guy. Jesus did not merely say he was rebuking the devil, He actually rebuked the devil by casting it out.

But it does not always have to be a case of demon possession. Sometimes, the devil may be clearly at work in other people without fully demonizing them, and we may rebuke the underlying spirit. For example, Peter was not demon-possessed when he tried to discourage Jesus from going to the cross. Yet Jesus looked in his direction and rebuked the devil.

> *But He turned and <u>said to Peter</u>, "Get behind Me, Satan! You are an offense to Me, for you are not mindful of the things of God, but the things of men." … (Matthew 16:23, emphasis mine)*

But if the problem you are facing is not demon-related, then what is there to rebuke or cast out? There are times you have to resist the devil, times when you have to wrestle against the devil, and times when you just have to be alert and aware of his devices. Not every problem can be solved by rebuking the devil.

How should we pray?

I know that what I have written in these two chapters will make a lot of people self-conscious when they pray. I don't want to do that. For some people, binding the devil is just terminology because that's how they learned to pray. So when they say *"I bind you devil"*, in their heart of hearts, they mean the same thing as *"Lord deliver us from the evil one"*. The second one is scriptural, the first one is not. But don't worry, God knows your heart. He knows if you are just using the wrong words or if you're actually trying to use authority that does not belong to you. But I have to teach what the Bible teaches, not what popular Christian culture teaches.

Jesus anticipated that one day, there would be a lot of myths going around causing people to pray amiss. That is why He taught us how to pray. He did not leave it to chance. Look at how Jesus Himself prayed at the tomb of Lazarus who was dead for four days.

> *Jesus lifted up His eyes and said, "Father, I thank You that You have heard Me. And I know that You always hear Me, but because of the people who are standing by I said this, that they may believe that You sent Me." ... Now when He had said these things, He cried with a loud voice, "Lazarus, come forth!" ... (John 11:41-43)*

Notice how Jesus first conversed with His Father, then commanded Lazarus to come forth. He prayed first, then He used His authority. Notice also that He did not bind the spirit of death. There are things we need to take to God in prayer, and there are times we need to use the authority Christ has given us. If there is a demon at work in somebody's life, pray to your Father, then rebuke the demon, command it to go in Jesus' name. If someone is sick, pray the way the apostles prayed, *"Be healed in Jesus' name"*.

> *Then Peter said, "Silver and gold I do not have, but what I do have I give you: In the name of Jesus Christ of Nazareth, <u>rise up and walk</u>." ... (Acts 3:6, emphasis mine)*

> *And Peter said to him, "Aeneas, Jesus the Christ heals you. <u>Arise and make your bed</u>." Then he arose immediately ... (Acts 9:34, emphasis mine)*

> *Paul, observing him intently and seeing that he had faith to be healed, said with a loud voice, "<u>Stand up straight on your feet</u>!" And he leaped and walked ... (Acts 14:9-10, emphasis mine)*

If you have an unsaved loved one, the Bible says that their eyes have been blinded by the prince of this age *(2 Corinthians 4:4)*. They are under demonic attack and don't even realize it. This can inform us how to pray for them. Pray for conviction by the Holy Spirit. Pray for God to open their eyes. Then let the blinding demon know what the Word of God says.

> *"Lord I pray that you will open the eyes of my unsaved loved ones through the convicting power of the Holy Spirit. Soften their heart and draw them to you in true repentance."*

> *"Demon, the Word of God tells me that you are blinding the eyes of my unsaved loved ones, but the Word of God also says that Jesus is the light of the world, the gospel is the power of God unto salvation, and God desires all to be saved and come to the knowledge of the truth. You are powerless against the gospel because the Author of the New Covenant is the same one who crushed your head on Calvary 2000 years ago, and the Bible declares that the same Spirit that raised Christ from the dead lives in me."*

Notice how this prayer uses the Word of God as a sword. Notice how much deeper this is than *"I bind you blinding spirit, I loose eye sight in Jesus' name."* Depending on how you phonate on the words *"bind"* and *"loose"*, they may sound like warfare words, but they are not. The example above is much more authoritative because it is based on the Word of God. Authority does not reside in your tone of voice, but in the Word of God.

There are other times when you cannot really rebuke the devil with words. For example if you give to the Lord, <u>He</u> will rebuke the devourer.

> *Bring all the tithes into the storehouse ... And <u>I will rebuke the devourer</u> for your sakes ... (Malachi 3:10-11, emphasis mine)*

Sometimes, you just have to leave it in God's hands.

> *Yet Michael the archangel, in contending with the devil, when he disputed about the body of Moses, dared not bring against him a reviling accusation, but said, "<u>The Lord rebuke you</u>!" ... (Jude 9, emphasis mine)*

There are times when there is no devil to rebuke. If there are temptations, you need to resist the devil. If there are trials, you have to endure. If you find yourself committing sin over and over, you need to confess your sin and crucify the flesh, not bind or rebuke the devil *(more on that in chapter 11)*. Look at how the apostles prayed when they were being threatened by the Sanhedrin. Do you see any place in these verses where they tried to bind any prevailing spirit?

> *"Lord, You are God, who made heaven and earth and the sea, and all that is in them ... For truly against Your holy Servant Jesus, whom You anointed, both Herod and Pontius Pilate, with the Gentiles and the people of Israel, were gathered together to do whatever Your hand and Your purpose determined before to be done.*
>
> *Now, Lord, look on their threats, and grant to Your servants that with all boldness they may speak Your word, by stretching out Your hand to heal, and that signs and wonders may be done through the name of Your holy Servant Jesus."*
>
> *... Acts 4:24-30*

Cry out to God

A few years ago, there were some co-workers trying to get me fired. One of them was the brother of the CEO, who was vying for a top position. For some reason he thought I did not support him, and he wanted me out. I was not just imagining this. I spoke with other high ranking officials who told me that I needed to watch my back. He was looking for any document with my signature that he could use against me.

Now this guy was the brother of the CEO, and the CEO was appointed by a representative of the government. I was powerless against them. 80 people had just been fired in what was considered a major case of political cleansing. Everyone in the organization was on edge. I was married just over a year and could not afford to lose my job, but it was in danger.

I spent quite a few sleepless nights praying and fasting. I cried out to God. I started reading and praying all the Psalms, and a few verses from Psalm 31 jumped out at me.

> *For I hear the slander of many; Fear is on every side; while they take counsel together against me, they scheme to take away my life. But as for me, I trust in You, O Lord; I say, "You are my God." My times are in Your hand; Deliver me from the hand of my enemies, And from those who persecute me.*
>
> *Make Your face shine upon Your servant; save me for Your mercies' sake. Do not let me be ashamed, O Lord, for I have called upon You; Let the wicked be*

ashamed; Let them be silent in the grave. Let the lying lips be put to silence, which speak insolent things proudly and contemptuously against the righteous.

... Psalm 31:13-18

It did not just say my life is in God's hands, but my times. I took that to God in prayer.

"Lord, you see how these people are making themselves my enemies without cause. They take counsel together against me. They have great political power, but as for me, I trust in you. My life and times are in your hands. You don't just determine whether I live or die, but every aspect of my life. You gave me this job and you determine whether I keep it or lose it. You are in control not them. Regardless of their political power, they are not God. They act like God, but they are not God. Lord flex your muscles and show them who is God. Lord make my enemies your enemies and fight against them."

Within a couple of months, a major scandal was uncovered involving the CEO and one of his secretaries. The CEO was fired on the spot, and his brother *(who wanted me fired)* was forced to resign. A couple of years later, he got sick and died. I am not gloating. I had long forgiven him and was actually sad when he died.

At no point did I feel the need to bind the devil. I did recognize that there were demons at work through these individuals, and I did rebuke them by letting them know what the Word of God said. But mostly, I threw myself at the mercy of God and humbly allowed Him to fight for me. I prayed the way Jesus taught me to pray *"Deliver us from the evil one"*. I prayed like the psalmists *"I cried unto the Lord and he heard me and delivered me."* God delivered me from the hands of bloodthirsty men, and God gave me the victory.

That's how I advise you to pray. Whatever trial you are going through, open up the Psalms. I am sure you will find something in there that is similar to what you are going through. Study it. Meditate on it. Pray the Psalms. Most importantly, pray, fast and cry out to God.

There is something powerful about crying out to God in desperation. Over and over in the Psalms, the psalmist cried out to God and God heard and delivered. Crying out to God is one of the most powerful prayers you could pray.

Ahab and Manasseh were two of the most wicked kings in the Old Testament. They forsook God and did not walk in His ways. But when both of them found themselves in trouble, they humbled themselves and cried out to God. Amazingly, God did not turn His nose up at them. He heard them and delivered them. You can read their stories in 1 Kings 21 and 2 Chronicles 33.

If God would hear wicked people when they cry to Him, how much more would He hear you, His child, when you cry out? This is how powerful it is when we cry out to God. Instead of binding and loosing, try crying out to Him instead. Instead of presuming authority that rightly belongs to God and God alone, try humbling yourself before God. The Bible says God resists the proud (*1 Peter 5:5*).

Do you feel like God is resisting your prayers? Check to see if there is pride. Pride does not always mean turning up your nose. Pride sometimes means thinking more of yourself than is merited. It could be that you are spending so much time binding and loosing, that God is just backing off and letting you have your way. In contrast, Psalm 51:17 says the sacrifices of God are a broken and a contrite heart.

Instead, why don't you back off and let God have His way? Humble yourself before God. Cry out to God. Forget about binding and loosing. Stop following these new teachings. Ask and you shall receive, seek and you shall find. That is what the Bible teaches. Try it.

MYTH #4

I THINK I HAVE A DEMON

How this myth keeps us in bondage

This myth creates an imaginary world where the devil is big and God is small. We act as though the devil is in control and we attribute every difficulty we face to a demon. We essentially give the devil the glory for every bad thing that happens.

What you will learn in the next two chapters

- Christians do not need deliverance from demons
- What the devil can and cannot do
- Witchcraft cannot work against Christians
- Deliverance comes from knowledge and understanding of the truth, not from the laying of hands

Let the truth free you from the burden of constantly believing that some demon or act of witchcraft can have any kind of control over you.

CHAPTER 7

CAN CHRISTIANS HAVE DEMONS?

How do I get that Benny Hinn anointing?

When I was just saved, I used to watch Benn Hinn on TV. As he laid hands on people they would fall. Sometimes he would wave at people and they would fall. I even heard one time that he threw his jacket into the crowd and people fell. I wanted that power. I thought how cool it would be if I had that power. I wouldn't even need martial arts. A burglar breaks into my house, WHAM! He gets slain in the Spirit while I call 911. Of course, this was not just for my own selfish amusement. While he is on the ground doing carpet time, the Holy Spirit would minister to him so that he would get saved even before the police showed up.

Like most new Christians, I did not know much about Christianity or the Bible. I would just go by what other people said or what I observed. But unlike most Christians, I studied the Bible for myself and eventually got delivered from Christian mythology.

Nevertheless, during my early Christian days, I really wanted that spectacular demonstration of God's power in my life. I tried to put the pieces together. Why was it that Benny Hinn and Morris Cerullo could demonstrate that kind of power, but I couldn't? I searched the scriptures and could not find an answer that fit into my existing framework. So I tried to postulate theories why I did not have the Benny Hinn anointing.

Then I heard a deliverance minister say that all Christians have demons and need deliverance. According to him, we may not have the frothing manifesting demons, but we have demons. Then a light bulb went on. I finally figured it out. With this new information, I came to the conclusion that the reason I did not have the Benny Hinn anointing was because of some little itty bitty demon hidden away in some small crevice of my spirit. I knew that I had the Holy Spirit, but I also thought there was some stubborn little demon hiding in there. I even gave it a name – a squatting spirit. I postulated that if I could get that little demon cast out, then that

Benny Hinn anointing could flow freely. Thank God I was not preaching as yet.

So I found a renowned deliverance church, attended a service and went to the altar after the sermon. Guess what happened. Absolutely nothing! I did not need deliverance from any demon because there was no demon.

After having studied the scriptures, I am convinced that Christians cannot have demons living in them. That deliverance minister was, respectfully, wrong. Christians could get delivered from a lot of things – trials, persecution, sin, fear, the body of death – but not demons. Born again children of God have the Holy Spirit living in them. No demon could live there. Demons could do other things, but they cannot possess or inhabit a child of God.

God is bigger than demons

Many Christians are in bondage just like I was. Their bondage is caused not by demons, but by incorrect beliefs – myths. Think about it. If a demon could prevent the Holy Spirit from manifesting His full power, doesn't that imply that the demon is bigger than the Holy Spirit. So according to this myth, even the little demons are bigger than God. This is another God-limiting myth that keeps Christians in bondage.

Whenever they go through any kind of trial, they assume that there is some demon responsible for it. If they are sick, it is a spirit of infirmity. If they are afraid, it is a spirit of fear. If they are going through difficult circumstances, somebody worked witchcraft on them. They think about anyone who does not like them, and they believe that person worked voodoo on them.

There is a joke about the devil sitting outside a church crying. So someone asked, *"Hey little guy, why are you crying?"* The devil replied, *"These Christians are blaming me for everything. AND STOP CALLING ME LITTLE!"*

When we blame the devil for everything, we are actually giving him more credit than he deserves. We are attributing God's glory to the devil, because believe it or not, God is responsible for and in control of the trials you face.

I will show you from the scriptures that God is big. The devil does not hinder God. In fact, God controls the devil and He even uses the devil to get His work done. The devil is like a puppet and God pulls his strings. The devil may hinder us sometimes, but he never hinders God. Our God is big. The devil is small. Instead of focusing on the devil, start focusing on God.

Start focusing on how big your God is. As you magnify God in your mind, all of these problems will immediately become small and fall in perspective.

My haunted house

We have a house that we only occupied on weekends. A few years ago, we decided that it made more economical sense to rent it out. So we put an ad and got tenants. Within a few weeks, the tenants complained that there was *"something"* in the house. It felt like some kind of presence in the house with them. This *"something"* would actually play with their kids. On one occasion as they entered the house after a day out, their daughter immediately started to run up the stairs. *"Hey, where are you going?"* they asked her. She replied, *"My friend is calling me upstairs."* They were puzzled because there was no friend in the house. Their daughter saw and played with this friend frequently. They also claimed that their son's eyes would turn eerily black. Our friends thought they were crazy. Eventually they moved out.

We got another tenant, but did not mention anything to her about what had happened to the previous tenants. Within one day, she was out of there. She spent one night, and she claimed that something had held her down for the entire night. She refused to go into details, although it really wasn't that hard to figure out.

Then we recalled an earlier house guest who had claimed to have seen the imprint of some invisible entity rolling on the bed. We had commanded whatever it was to leave in Jesus' name, and there was no problem after that. This was before the tenants started reporting problems.

So after three independent sets of people complained about what Hollywood calls *"paranormal activity"*, we figured they could not all be crazy. We prayed and fasted, we called in other ministers who were also experienced and gifted to deal with demons. Today, the house is occupied by a wonderful born-again family who has never complained about a single incident of demonic interference.

We marvel over the fact that we occupied that house for years before the tenants, and we never had a problem with demons. The Bible does not tell us a lot about demons simply because we do not need to know where they came from or what their names are. We only need to know that God has given us authority over them, and they can by no means harm us.

This experience has taught us that born-again children of God walk in a higher realm than unsaved people. The same demons that terrorized and tormented unbelievers were powerless against Christians. This experience is consistent with scripture. The Bible teaches that we have been raised up to sit with Christ in heavenly places above principalities and powers (*Ephesians*

2:6 cf. 1:20-21). God has given us the victory over demons. Trust me, demons cannot possess or inhabit Christians. Our God is too big.

What exactly can the devil do?

There are many cases of demon possession in the Bible. Not a single one of them involved born-again Christians. Some deliverance ministers differentiate between demon possession and demonic oppression, but the Bible does not recognize any such distinction. The Bible uses the Greek word, *daimonizomenous*, which means to be demonized. Sometimes it is translated as *"demon-possessed"* (*Matthew 8:16*) or *"had a spirit of an unclean demon"* (*Luke 4:33*). Demon-possession is also called demonic oppression (*see Acts 10:38*).

When someone is demonized, they fall under the control of the demon. They do things that they do not intend to do. They cut themselves, or throw themselves in fire. Sometimes, they display feats of strength that humans do not normally have. All of these things are consistent with scripture as well as the experiences of many deliverance ministers. These people are demonized. You could call it oppression, possession or you could simply say they have a demon.

This cannot happen to Christians. There is no precedent of it happening to any Christian in the Bible. Mary Magdalene had seven demons cast out of her. But after she walked with Christ, she never again had a problem with demons. Even after Christ ascended into heaven, every case of demon possession that the apostles encountered involved people who were not (yet) born-again.

Of course, this does not mean that the devil can do nothing. There are things he can do, but possessing Christians is not one of them.
1) He can tempt us (*Mark 1:13*)
2) He can hinder us (*1 Thessalonians 2:18*)
3) He can buffet us (*2 Corinthians 12:7*)
4) He can deceive us (*2 Corinthians 11:3*)
5) He can accuse us before God – rightfully or wrongfully (*Revelation 12:10*)

Christians do not need deliverance from demons. But they could use deliverance from many other things. For example, the psalmist spoke of God delivering him from fear, from destruction, and from a horrible pit. Paul talked about himself being delivered from the body of death (*Romans 7:24*). But no one in the Bible ever spoke about Christians being delivered from demonization. It is simply not something that Christians need to worry about, yet so many of us do. We *"cover ourselves in the blood"* during deliverances because we are cautious of demons coming on us when they are cast out. This is needless bondage.

Deliverance vs. discipleship

We can learn a lot from the Apostle Paul on how to pray when difficult situations arise.

> *And lest I should be exalted above measure by the abundance of the revelations, a thorn in the flesh was given to me, a messenger of Satan to buffet me ... Concerning this thing I pleaded with the Lord three times that it might depart from me.*
>
> *And He said to me, "My grace is sufficient for you, for My strength is made perfect in weakness." Therefore most gladly I will rather boast in my infirmities, that the power of Christ may rest upon me. Therefore I take pleasure in infirmities, in reproaches, in needs, in persecutions, in distresses, for Christ's sake. For when I am weak, then I am strong.*
>
> *... 2 Corinthians 12:7-10*

Paul was given a thorn in the flesh. This was not a literal thorn, otherwise he could have just squeezed it out. It was a messenger of Satan sent to buffet him. Now that does not sound good. Whether the buffeting part was literal or figurative, we can only speculate. Some people believe that Paul was talking about a sickness that he had, others (including myself) believe he was referring to the non-stop trials that followed him everywhere he went. But whatever it was, it was not pleasant.

So Paul prayed for deliverance. Three times he prayed to God to deliver him from that situation. Notice that the first thing Paul did was not bind, cast out or rebuke the devil. He did not exclaim, *"THE DEVIL IS A LIAR!"* That's <u>not</u> how Paul approached the problem. He prayed to God. He recognized that God is big and God is in control. He did not give the devil the credit or the glory. He did not make the devil bigger than he really was. He prayed to God for deliverance.

God then told him, *"My grace is sufficient for you, my strength is made perfect in your weakness."* This was just a nice way of saying,

> *"NOPE. I am not going to deliver you from this. If I take it away, you will get puffed up with pride. I know you better than you know yourself Paul, and I know what is best for you even though you don't realize it."*

God chose not to deliver Paul from that situation. There are some trials that God will deliver you from, and some He won't. God never promised a trouble-free life. In fact He expressly told us not to be surprised when trials come *(1 Peter 4:12)*. Paul prayed for deliverance, but instead God gave him understanding. Paul thought he needed deliverance, but he really needed knowledge.

Paul wrote many epistles in the New Testament. Almost all of them were written in response to some situation or problem that the believers faced. He did not blame the devil or bind the devil when a problem arose. He did not invite the Christians to his deliverance center. He wrote to them. By the very act of writing letters, Paul acknowledged that what these believers needed was not deliverance, but instruction in righteousness. The same is true of us. We often think we need deliverance, but what we really need is teaching. What we really need is discipleship. This is an old-fashioned word that is not used anymore. But it is actually part of the Great Commission.

> *Go therefore and make disciples of all the nations ... (Matthew 28:19, emphasis mine)*

We are to evangelize the world by preaching the gospel and making disciples of all nations. The unsaved need to hear the gospel to get saved, then when they get saved they need to be taught and discipled. Do not underestimate the importance of teaching in your Christian walk. Teaching was an integral aspect of the early church, yet overlooked by so many today.

> *And they continued steadfastly in the apostles' doctrine and fellowship, in the breaking of bread, and in prayers ... (Acts 2:42)*

What do we do whenever we have a problem? We wait until the end of the sermon, then go to the altar for prayer. There is nothing wrong with this per se, but it does reveal that we place a higher value on deliverance than on discipleship. Our priorities are reversed. The greater emphasis should be on the teaching of the Word of God. That is what equips us with what we need to mature and grow as Christians. That is what provides us with the truth that sets us free.

Get understanding

> *When anyone hears the word of the kingdom, and does not understand it, then the wicked one comes and snatches away what was sown in his heart. This is he*

who received seed by the wayside. ... But he who received seed on the good ground is he who hears the word and <u>understands</u> it, who indeed bears fruit and produces: some a hundredfold, some sixty, some thirty. ... (Matthew 13:19, 23, emphasis mine)

In the most fundamental parable of the kingdom of God, Jesus likened the kingdom to a man sowing seeds. The seed of course is the Word of God, and it falls on different kinds of soil. The stony ground refers to believers who hear the word and <u>do not understand</u>. The devil can then easily steal the word from them. Then they complain about the devil and they seek deliverance, when what they really need is understanding. The good soil refers to believers who hear the word and <u>understand</u>. You don't need deliverance, you need understanding.

Whatever situation you are going through, stop giving the devil the glory for it. God is in control, and if there is any demon at work, it is because God has allowed it. Instead of focusing on the demon, go a few steps higher and seek God instead. The deliverance minister will tell you to identify the demon at work, find out his name, and then you can cast it out. But what the Bible says you need is knowledge and understanding.

Corporate America spends over 50 billion dollars every year in management consulting fees. All consultants do is provide information. These businesses obviously think that knowledge is a crucial ingredient in their success. You have the Word of God which is sharper than a two-edged sword. God exalted His Word above His own Name (*Psalm 138:2*). Do you believe there is power in the name of Jesus? Well there is power in the Word of God. Use it!

In the next chapter, we will continue this thought by addressing another related issue – can witchcraft work against Christians? Are your problems in life the result of someone working witchcraft on you?

CHAPTER 8

CAN WITCHCRAFT WORK AGAINST CHRISTIANS?

In the last chapter, we learned that Christians cannot be possessed by demons. In this chapter, we will look at a more specific form of demonic activity and one that Christians tend to worry about a lot – witchcraft.

Let me start off by saying that witchcraft is real. There are real witches and voodoo priests out there. In some countries, they are called *"obeah men"*. There are many powerful people in society who got where they are because of pacts they made with the devil. There are witchdoctors who use potions to help people win back lost love. I know some of these are gimmicks, but some are real – they actually deal in the occult.

When Christians go through trials, they sometimes remember everyone who does not or might not like them – whether a coworker, a neighbor, or a *"friend"*. Then they try to put the pieces together, and in their finite understanding, they are convinced that someone worked witchcraft against them. They then go through a process of cancelling the witchcraft and sending it back. <u>None of that is necessary because Christians are automatically protected</u>.

The devil looked at Job but could not get anywhere near him because God had placed a hedge around his person, his family, his health, and his possessions *(Job 1:10)*. As righteous as Job was, if you are a born-again Christian, you have the very righteousness of Christ. You also have that hedge of protection. You have the armor of God that protects you from the wiles of the devil. If the devil cannot touch you on his own, do you think he can touch you if another human being invokes him? It makes no sense.

I know a pastor who had a confrontation with an obeah man. The obeah man threatened to put a spell on him and destroy him. The pastor knew he was protected in Christ and had angels encamped around him. He was not in the least bit worried. In a few months, that obeah man got really sick. In the pastor's own words, an ambulance showed up at the obeah man's house, took him to the hospital, and he never came back.

I know of another pastor who was approached by a male witch, who told him that he tried for years to *"astral project"* to bring a curse upon the pastor, but to no avail. He was able to do that successfully against others, but not the pastor because there was a shield that he could not penetrate. God used this experience to bring the witch to his knees in repentance.

The only way the devil could have attacked Job was if God permitted the devil to do it. In his case, God permitted him to touch his family and his possessions, but not his person. Later on, God allowed the devil to attack Job's health, but not his life. God is in control.

Witchcraft in the early church

On two occasions in the early church, the apostles had to deal with witchcraft. Simon the sorcerer astonished the people with his sorceries (*Acts 8:11*), yet when Peter confronted him, he ended up begging for mercy (*Acts 8:24*). Later on, Paul encountered another sorcerer, called Elymas, who was trying to undermine his work. Paul pronounced a curse on him and the sorcerer ended up blind (*Acts 13:11*). We see that the power of mighty sorcerers crumbled like sand next to the power of God.

Bring it on, Balaam

The children of Israel were a murmuring complaining bunch. God was angry with them in Numbers 21. God was angry with them in Numbers 25. Did I mention that God was angry with them? But right there in between, in Numbers 22-24, there is a story of a man called Balak who wanted to curse Israel. He hired a *"prophet"* called Balaam. The description of Balaam suggests that he was a witchdoctor. Joshua 13:22 calls him a soothsayer. He was the real deal. He was not one of those horoscope prophets telling your fortune by cold-reading you. He was a "real false prophet". He was very much in touch with the spiritual realm, and he was good at what he did.

Four times he tried to curse Israel and four times God forced him to bless them. <u>As good as Balaam was, and as bad as the children of Israel were, the only thing that mattered was how big the God of Israel is</u>. Balaam said he could not curse whom God had blessed because the shout of a king was among them. Do you still think witchcraft could work against you? You don't understand how big your God is.

But the witchcraft is actually working against me...

That's just what you think. That's just how you interpret your situation with your limited understanding. There are a number of reasons why witchcraft may <u>appear</u> to be working.

You are not genuinely saved
Check yourself. It does not matter if you have church membership or not. Are you born-again? Has your life been changed from an old creature to a new one? If you are not saved, then witchcraft can work against you.

It is something other than witchcraft
If you are saved, then what you are experiencing is most likely not witchcraft. It may be regular trials that you are going through, and you just think it is witchcraft because of what other people told you. God is allowing trials, and maybe He is using the devil to accomplish parts of it. Instead of recognizing that God is the one in control, you are attributing the problem to the devil. You are making the devil big and God small.

You have committed some sin for which God is chastening you
After Balaam realized he was unable to curse Israel, he instructed Balak to send the women of Moab to tempt the men of Israel into sexual sin. When this happened, Israel incurred God's wrath. So as far as Balaam was concerned, the end result was the same. Check your life for unconfessed sin. Perhaps you are being chastened by God and mistaking it for witchcraft.

Lack of knowledge
Sometimes simply getting knowledge can make a lot of problems go away. After all knowing the truth is what sets you free. Witchcraft and eating food offered to idols are very similar. In fact, making potions over food is a favorite among voodoo practitioners. Here is what Paul said in 1 Corinthians 8.

> *Therefore concerning the eating of things offered to idols, <u>we know</u> that <u>an idol is nothing</u> in the world, and that <u>there is no other God but one</u>. ... However, <u>there is not in everyone that knowledge</u>; for some, with consciousness of the idol, until now eat it as a thing offered to an idol; and <u>their conscience, being weak, is defiled</u> ... (1 Corinthians 8:4, 7, emphasis mine)*

The truth is that there is one God and an idol is nothing. But if you lack that knowledge, it can lead to bondage. When you fail to see how big God is, it can lead to bondage. The devil thrives on ignorance. We are destroyed for lack of knowledge. Once you get that knowledge in you, somehow it lifts you to a higher state where these spiritual problems no longer bother you.

How Gehazzi got delivered from fear

Gehazzi, Elisha's servant, also failed to recognize how big God is. On one occasion, he and Elisha were surrounded by the Syrian army on every side, and Gehazzi was terrified. Elisha recognized that a spirit of fear is not a demon spirit called fear, but rather a condition where the human spirit is paralyzed by fear. Elisha realized that Gehazzi did not need deliverance from any demon spirit of fear, but instead what he needed was an understanding of how big his God was. So Elisha assured him that *"those who are with us are more than those who are with them"* and he prayed for God to open his eyes (*2 Kings 6:16-17*). When Gehazzi's eyes were opened, he looked up, and this time he did not just see the Syrian army surrounding them, but he saw God's chariots of fire surrounding the enemy. In that moment, I am sure that Gehazzi's fear was eviscerated.

Once you realize how big God is, it is impossible to continue to live in fear. Once you realize how big God is, witchcraft loses its hold on you.

What are you going through? I am almost certain that if I could diagnose your problem, somewhere along the line, I would find that you do not quite understand how big God is. Are you sick? Well God is Jehovah Rapha our healer. Are you afraid? The Bible says that demons believe in God and they tremble (*James 2:19*).

Think about what this means. <u>The demons that you think are so big and scary – they are terrified in the presence of God</u>. The demons that you think are being sent by someone to torment you – they are tormented by the very thought of God. How big do you think the devil is? God is infinitely bigger. You don't need deliverance from demons or witchcraft, you just need to understand how big God is.

How to pray for protection

Instead of binding everything that moves, casting out imaginary demons, breaking generational curses, sending back witchcraft, and pleading the blood over every square inch of space; there are many Biblical ways to pray for God's protection.

Put a hedge around me (Job 1:10)

Lord arise and let your enemies be scattered (Psalm 68:1)

Keep me in the secret place of the Most High, the shadow of the Almighty (Psalm 91:1)

Cover me and hide me under Your wings (Psalm 91:4)

Give Your angels charge over me (Psalm 91:11)

When the enemy comes in like a flood, lift up a standard against him (Isaiah 59:19)

Let no weapon formed against me prosper (Isaiah 54:17)

Deliver me from the evil one (Matthew 6:13)

What do you notice about all these prayers? They are directed to God, not against the devil. They operate under the assumption that God is big and the devil is small.

MYTH #5

I CAN LAY LOW AND AVOID THE DEVIL

How this myth keeps us in bondage

This myth creates a world in our minds where the devil is in control, not God. Instead of going boldly to God in prayer, it makes us very timid in our prayer, rendering our prayers ineffective.

What you will learn in the next two chapters

- God is in control, not the devil
- The devil is just a puppet God uses to fulfill His purposes
- God sends trials, not the devil
- Our prayers should not be too strategic, but bold, passionate and fervent

Let the truth free you from the burden of believing that the devil is in control, and that when trials come your way, it means that the devil is winning, and you and God are losing.

CHAPTER 9

WHO IS IN CONTROL – GOD OR THE DEVIL?

Shhh, the Devil is listening

I once heard a pastor tell his congregation that when they pray, they should pray in their minds.

> *The devil is not omniscient like God – he does not know everything – therefore he cannot know your thoughts. But if you pray out loud, the devil hears you, and he can unleash his forces against you. Instead you should pray in your mind, so the devil does not know what you're praying for, and does not know how to attack you.* [8]

This actually came as a shock to me because it went completely against the grain of Charismatic Christian culture. You are more likely to hear people teaching the opposite, that we should pray out loud and <u>not</u> in our minds. This is because most of these guys place a heavy emphasis on our words, so if you don't speak out loud, your prayers have no effect.

<u>Both</u> teachings are wrong. The truth is that God knows what you need long before you ask, so whether you pray in your mind or out loud makes no difference to God. The praying-in-your-mind myth makes the devil big and God small, while the praying-out-loud myth treats God as an impersonal principle that gets activated once we apply the right formula. Not only are these teachings wrong, they limit God.

If you pray in your mind to prevent the devil from hearing, you are essentially saying that your God is small and the devil is big, but you are working around it. You obviously won't come out openly and say that, and you certainly won't write a song about it. But you're doing just about everything else to communicate it. Why else would you be so afraid of the devil hearing your prayers? So what if the devil knows what you are praying for? He is not in control and he cannot do anything without God's permission. Ultimately, God is in control and He even controls the devil.

Teachings like these only serve to magnify the devil. Now even prayer becomes a source of bondage. Have you ever watched one of those Lifetime movies where the leading actress is trying to fight off the bad guy? During the struggle, the gun falls out the bad guy's hand, and she gets hold of it. She is now pointing the gun at the bad guy, and you're watching the movie and yelling at the screen *"Shoot him! Shoot!"* But her hands are trembling and she can't pull the trigger. The bad guy then walks over to her and takes back the gun.

Guess what, I just described you. You have a powerful weapon called prayer in your arsenal, but instead of using it as a weapon against the devil, these myths have made you timid even in your prayers. Talk about bondage.

There are two fundamental problems with these teachings.
1) They make God small and the devil big.
2) They assume that the devil is the one who sends trials, when in fact trials come from God.

I know that trials can be really heart-wrenching at times. We would do everything we could to avoid trials or to get over them as fast as we could. But I will show you that trials are not as bad as you think. There is a lot of good that can come out of trials if you allow God to have His way. Don't try to short-circuit what God is doing.

God has the trump cards

In Trinidad, there is a popular card game called *All Fours* which comprises four players – two teams of two players each. One of the key objectives in the game is to *"hang your opponent's Jack"*. What does that mean? In each round of play, a particular suit is trump (*spades, diamonds, etc.*). If you have the Jack in the trump suit, that puts you in a vulnerable position. If your opponents have a higher trump card – Queen, King or Ace – they can hang your Jack if they play their cards right. That is the ultimate embarrassment in All Fours, and it counts for a lot of points. Players will try to read any body language signal to figure out who has the Jack.

Once I was playing *All Fours* and I had the Jack. I was visibly nervous. I couldn't hide it. My opponents could see it written all over my face. They were using every strategy to get me to play the Jack at the wrong time so they could hang it. Eventually I capitulated. In what I thought was the most strategic move to save the Jack, I played it and my opponent hanged it with his King. As they celebrated and gloated, my partner yelled out at me, *"Why did you do that? I have the Ace!"*

Because the Ace is the highest card, he could have saved my Jack from being hanged. But I did not know he had the Ace. Normally in *All Fours*, you are supposed to communicate with your partner, which I obviously did not do. Why? Because my opponents were looking straight at me. I wanted to signal to my partner that I had the Jack, but I was afraid my opponents would see. The irony is that had I communicated with my partner anyway, he would have let me know that he had the Ace and that my Jack was safe. It did not matter if my opponents had found out.

Are you allowing the devil to hang your Jack, not realizing that God holds the Ace? This is precisely what happens when you pray timidly before God. If you understood how big your God is, you would never be afraid to let the devil hear your prayers. In fact, the devil would be the one afraid to hear your prayers. The real tragedy is not when the devil hears your prayers, but when God does not hear them.

Call 911 already!

In 2010, there was some really bad flash flooding in Nashville. It was described as a once in a thousand years event. 19 inches of rain fell in two days, and towns were flooded out. 21 persons perished in the floods. There was one particular survivor who survived in spite of her horrible judgment.

She was alone with her 4 year old daughter, when she noticed the floods coming into the house. Her car was already covered, and the water inside the house was now at the level of her sofa and rising rapidly. Appliances were floating. She sat on the kitchen counter holding her daughter.

Here is the ironic part. She had the phone in her hand. But in what has to be the worst logic of all time, she refused to call 911 because she did not want her daughter to hear the panic in her voice. In the end, someone else called 911 and she was rescued.[9]

When we hesitate to pray because we are afraid of the devil hearing, it is precisely the same thing. Perhaps you have been surviving on other people's prayers. But you can do much more than survive if you learn to pray for yourself, and go boldly to the throne of God.

Who is really in control?

When you give in to teachings that say we should pray in our minds so the devil will not hear us, you are implying that the devil is in control. Yes the devil is called the god of this age (*2 Corinthians 4:4*) and the prince of this world *(John 14:30)*, but that does not mean he is in control. It simply means that he has a strong influence on the ungodly elements in this world. This is why the anti-Christian elements in the world are so strong. But the devil is not in control.

The devil may be the god of this world, but Jesus Christ is King of kings and Lord of lords. The devil may be the god of this age, but Jesus is Alpha and Omega, the Beginning and the End. The devil may control spiritual wickedness in high places, but Jesus is seated in heavenly places above principalities and powers.

God is in control even over the devil. The devil can only do what God allows him to do. The devil needed permission from God to attack Job. Even when God gave the devil permission, He explicitly told him what he could and could not do *(Job 1:12)*. <u>The devil is like a bad dog on a leash, and God controls the length of that leash</u>. It was an *"evil spirit from the Lord"* that was upon King Saul *(1 Samuel 19:9, KJV)*. It was <u>God</u> who sent a lying spirit to deceive Ahab.

> *And the Lord said, 'Who will persuade Ahab to go up, that he may fall at Ramoth Gilead?'... Then a spirit came forward and stood before the Lord, and said, 'I will persuade him.'*
>
> *The Lord said to him, 'In what way?' So he said, 'I will go out and be a lying spirit in the mouth of all his prophets.' And the Lord said, 'You shall persuade him, and also prevail. Go out and do so.'*
>
> *... 1 Kings 22:20-22*

Consider these scriptures:

> *...the accuser of our brethren ... has been cast down ... Woe to the inhabitants of the earth and the sea! For the devil has come down to you, having great wrath, because he knows that he has a short time. ... (Revelation 12:10, 12)*

This one may not be as obvious as the others, but let us consider the implications of these two verses. They speak of a future time when Satan will be cast down from the heavens, and then he will unleash his wrath against the inhabitants of the earth. This means that at present, Satan is being hindered or restrained from doing this. So it is not the devil that is hindering God, it is God who is hindering the devil. God is constantly blocking the devil, pulling his leash, controlling his strings and making him do whatever needs to be done to fulfill God's purposes. Stop acting as though God is small and the devil is big. God is in control.

Did the devil really orchestrate Jesus' death?

Now allow me to really blow your mind. You probably think that the devil moved the chief priests to crucify Jesus. To an extent you are right, but that is not the fully story. You probably picture Jesus dying on the cross then descending into hell where the demons were rejoicing and celebrating over His dead body. But 3 days later, Jesus broke the shackles of death, hell and the grave, and rose victoriously from the dead. In so doing, he ruined the demons' party. I'm just guessing that's probably what you believe.

In your scenario, God is definitely big because He defeated Satan. But I will one-up you. God is even bigger than you think. Satan did <u>not</u> want Jesus to be crucified. He knew Jesus' death on the cross would be detrimental to his kingdom. He knew what that meant for our salvation. But he was forced by God against his will to tempt Judas and the high priests.

> *Then Satan entered Judas, surnamed Iscariot, who ... conferred with the chief priests and captains, how he might betray Him ... (Luke 22:3-4)*

The Bible clearly says that Satan entered Judas Iscariot so he would betray Christ. But this is <u>not</u> what Satan wanted. In Matthew 16, he tried to tempt Peter to dissuade Jesus from going to His death.

> *Jesus began to show to His disciples that He must go to Jerusalem, and suffer many things from the elders and chief priests and scribes, and be killed, and be raised the third day.*
>
> *Then Peter took Him aside and began to rebuke Him, saying, "Far be it from You, Lord; this shall not happen to You!"*
>
> *But He turned and said to Peter, "Get behind Me, Satan! You are an offense to Me, for you are not mindful of the things of God, but the things of men."*
>
> *... Matthew 16:21-23*

Why would Satan do this if he wanted Jesus dead? When Peter was filled with the Holy Spirit, he added a new perspective on what really happened.

> *For truly against Your holy Servant Jesus, whom You anointed, both Herod and Pontius Pilate, with the Gentiles and the people of Israel, were gathered together <u>to do whatever Your hand and Your purpose determined before to be done</u>. ... (Acts 4:27-28, emphasis mine)*

Satan was only doing what God determined in advance he would do. God forced Satan to participate in his own demise, and Satan could do nothing about it. Satan is merely a fallen angel, and angels exist to do God's bidding (*Psalm 103:20*). It appears that Satan is no better.

Isn't it clear from these scriptures who is in control? Then why are we afraid of the devil hearing our prayers? When we pray, the emphasis should be on whether God hears us, not the devil. Our focus should be on identifying if there are any hindrances to God hearing us. We should not be in the least concerned over the devil.

In the next chapter, we will see that you really cannot avoid trials by trying to lay low. It is God who sends trials not the devil. There is no point hiding from the devil.

CHAPTER 10

CAN WE REALLY AVOID TRIALS?

In the last chapter, we saw that God is in control and not the devil. Therefore we should not try to lay low and avoid the devil, but go boldly to God in prayer.

When you pray silently to prevent the devil from hearing, there is another subtle implication. You clearly believe that it is possible, at least to some extent, to lay low and fly below the devil's radar. Well you can't. Trust me, the devil knows who you are. He said, *"Jesus I know, Paul I know" (Acts 19:15).* If you are a child of God, the devil knows who you are. You can't hide. But why are you even trying to hide?

We have a friend whose parents are from Trinidad but she was born and raised in New York. She looks like a Trinidadian, but she speaks like an American. Whenever she visits Trinidad, she tries to blend in so no one will know she is a tourist, but people immediately recognize it. Then she acts all surprised, *"How did they know?"* Although she looks like everyone else, there is a conspicuous difference that people simply cannot miss.

We are foreigners in a strange land, do you really think you could sneak below the devil's radar and he wouldn't know? This is a spiritual war, and the devil's intelligence systems are up and running. He may be small, but he is not stupid. You cannot lay low and hope to avoid trials. That's just not how Christianity works.

God sends trials not the devil

Even if you try to hide from the devil, you can't hide from God. Ultimately, God is the one who sends trials our way. It is God who chastens us and He is the one who uses trials to purify us *(James 1:2-3).* It was God who initiated the conversation with the devil about Job. God was using the devil to bring trials against Job.

Then the Lord said to Satan, "Have you considered My servant Job?" ... (Job 1:8)

When my nephew was a child, he grew accustomed to me feeding him. But there came a time when he had to learn to use a spoon for himself. It took him quite a while to get the hang of it. He would constantly be missing his mouth so his food fell on the floor. Then he would look at me with a betrayed look that communicated so clearly, *"Why do you hate me?"* It was heartbreaking to watch a hungry child try to feed himself and fail. I desperately wanted to step in and feed him, but then he would never learn to do it for himself. It was painful, but he eventually learned. Had I kept bailing him out, he would have never learned. Was it because he sinned? Was it because he did something wrong? Were we punishing him? No. There was a greater purpose that he could not possibly understand at the time.

... whom the Lord loves He chastens ... that we may be partakers of His holiness. ... (Hebrews 12:5, 10)

Whenever we have trials, we tend to wonder what we did wrong. Most likely you did nothing wrong. It is when you don't have trials, then you need to worry. God sends trials for a purpose. That purpose may not always be evident to us. But God uses trials to shape us and make us into what He called us to be. If God forced Satan to participate in the death of His only begotten Son, do you really think His master plan is to give you an easy life?

I lived in Miami for five years while I was pursuing my PhD. Unlike New York where everyone takes the subway and public buses, in Miami everyone drives. Only the crazies take the bus. If you use public transport in Miami and you paid for my book, I am not talking about you OK. It's the other people who are crazy.

During these five years, I made a decision to live very humbly since I was earning a very small stipend. I lived in a rundown little apartment that I rented for $300/month. On numerous occasions, I had to fight off rats and roaches. But the rent was affordable. I chose to not have a car since the cost of auto insurance was insane. I took the bus to and from school. I took the bus to the mall. I even took the bus to the laundry with my dirty clothes in a hamper. In the sweltering Miami heat or in torrential summer rain, I took the bus wherever I needed to go.

My apartment was a 10-minute walk from a local Publix (*a supermarket chain*). Every Friday evening, I would walk to the supermarket with my knapsack, do my shopping, then put all my groceries in my bag and walk back to my apartment. Whatever could not fit in the bag, I held in my hands. While everyone else was driving, I was one of the crazies walking from the supermarket with my groceries. In fact, the only thing that would have been more crazy is if I had pushed the shopping cart home.

That was my life for five years. I was one of the crazies living with the crazies in Miami. But this was the life I had chosen. I made a choice to live humbly because I did not want to go into debt by spending more than I earned. I also knew that if I got too comfortable, my studies would suffer. <u>I needed just enough discomfort to keep me on my toes and to keep me from complacency</u>. My goal was to finish my PhD on time, not to get comfortable.

The same thing is true of our walk with Christ. We are here on earth to complete a mission, not to get comfortable. So instead of trying to hide from trials, just accept them as part of your Christian walk. Paul said that our present distress is nothing compared to our future glory. The old hymn echoes that thought: *"Just one glimpse of Him in glory, will the toils of life repay."* [10]

<u>I surrender all</u>

Everyone would like to have a nice comfortable life here on earth. But that is not always God's will. In fact it is rarely God's will. The Christian walk is a life of trials, death and self-denial. Jesus said whoever comes to Him must deny himself, take up his cross and follow. Jesus Himself was a man of sorrows, acquainted with grief. He never promised us an easy life.

We run into problems when we get too attached to this life. Modern Christianity has become so materialistic that we associate material blessings with the favor of God, and then get upset with God if we do not attain wealth. Jesus said it is possible to gain the whole world and lose your soul. So how is material blessing a sign of God's favor? It makes no logical sense. God does bless us with nice things, but He is not going to give us everything we want.

Christianity is <u>not</u> a path to wealth and riches. Christianity is a life of self-denial. It is a life of dying daily. It is a life of daily surrender to God, which can be heart-wrenching at times. We are often called to give up the things we treasure the most. Johnson Oatman wrote,

> *Here the dearest of ties we must sever*
>
> *Tears of sorrow are seen everyday*
>
> *But no sickness, no sighing forever*
>
> *When I've gone the last mile of the way* [11]

This is a life where we agree to lose now so we can gain in the next life. The Apostle Paul echoed those sentiments,

> *But none of these things move me; nor do I count my life dear to myself, so that I may finish my race with joy, and the ministry which I received from the Lord Jesus, to testify to the gospel of the grace of God ... (Acts 20:24)*

I spoke on this topic in a church in Florida, noting that if God is going to do anything great in our lives, it would come through trials. A young man asked me during the Q&A session, *"How do we get trials?"* He reminded me of my younger self, eager to get over the trials as fast as I could so God could use me. A few years and many trials older, I just smiled and told him, *"Don't worry about getting trials. God will take care of that for you."*

Make the devil regret he ever messed with you

The apostle Paul had the right attitude toward trials. There was a time when he and Silas praised and worshiped God in a jail cell, and God orchestrated a miraculous jail break *(Acts 16:25-26)*. Maybe Paul might have been tempted to think that whenever the devil sends trials, God would miraculously show up and save the day. But this only happened <u>once</u> in Paul's life.

There were several other times Paul was thrown in prison, and God did not open the doors. God did not send any angel or earthquake to help Paul out. Perhaps Paul had his moments when he began to doubt.

> *"I used to have the anointing so strong, God would just open prison doors for me. Now that has dried up. Has God forsaken me and left me to rot in this jail cell? What did I do wrong?"*

Maybe Paul had his momentary pity-party, but I am sure he quickly shook it off. For a missionary like Paul, being thrown in jail was the absolute worst thing that could happen. He was supposed to be out there preaching the gospel, but instead he had to sit by himself in jail. How could that trial possibly be for God's glory? Here is what Paul did.

He realized he could not preach. So he got out a pen and some paper, and he started to write. He wrote letters to the Ephesians, Philippians, and Colossians all while in prison. Paul preached many sermons in his life, but most of them were never recorded, therefore we will never hear them. But every Christian in every generation could open up the Bible and read the sermons that Paul wrote while he was in jail. We find encouragement that

"I can do all things through Christ who strengthens me". We find assurance that *"God will supply all our needs according to His riches in glory"*. We learn that *"God is able to do exceedingly abundantly above all that we can ask or think"*, therefore we should *"set our affections on things above, and not things of the earth"*.

Prison prevented Paul from traveling to preach the gospel there and then, but through his chains, God accomplished an infinitely greater purpose. Paul has been dead for nearly 2000 years, but he is still preaching. His messages have blessed more people than Paul could have ever dreamed of reaching during his lifetime. I am sure that every time the gospel is preached, the devil regrets the day he messed with the Apostle Paul. Take that attitude toward trials. Make the devil rue the day he chose to mess with you.

The Bible tells us that the devil is like a roaring lion seeking whom he may devour *(1 Peter 5:8)*. Lions are strategic pack hunters. There is one particular strategy that I find interesting. After scoping out a herd of buffalo or antelope, the lions would send the oldest slowest lion to the front of the herd while the other lions wait in ambush. The old lion would roar with the sole intention of scaring the herd. When the herd hears the roar, their natural instinct is to run in the opposite direction – directly into the ambush.

Don't run from the devil, run straight toward him. Don't be afraid of the devil, make him scared of you. You are a child of the most high God, the Greater One is in you than the devil who is in the world, and if God is for you who could be against you? Pray and ask God how He can help you turn around your trial for His glory. Ask God to give you a testimony that can bless other people when it is over.

MYTH #6

THE DEVIL MADE ME DO IT

How this myth keeps us in bondage

This myth makes the devil bigger than he really is not realizing that Satan is only as powerful as our flesh would allow him. The devil uses our flesh to tempt us to sin, and we are thus unable to stand before God with a clear conscience. We focus on attacking the devil when we should be attacking our flesh, and as a result we remain in bondage.

What you will learn in the next two chapters

- Our weapons of warfare are not for destroying the devil's kingdom, but for pulling down strongholds
- The strongholds of the devil are in our minds
- How to wage a good warfare
- How real life Christians overcame strongholds in their own lives

Let the truth free you from the burden of believing that you have to be constantly fighting the devil, waging the wrong warfare and missing the mark.

CHAPTER 11

WHAT ARE STRONGHOLDS?

How Snuffleupagus ended up on Sesame Street

If you watched Sesame Street in my era, you would have probably grown up believing that elephants are gentle peace-loving creatures who hang out with big birds, and speak with a deep grainy voice that makes them sound clinically depressed. This could not be further from the truth.

Elephants are ferocious beasts. They are not carnivores, so they don't eat people. But they can be vicious especially when breeding. I have seen videos of elephants overturning safari vehicles with their tusks. I have read accounts of elephants lifting up hunters with their trunks and crushing them under their heavy weight. I am not in any way advocating cruelty to elephants, I am simply making the point that elephants are not tame. They are wild.

Have you ever wondered how they capture elephants? Elephants are native to the jungles of South Asia and the plains of Africa. How do they end up in zoos and circuses all over the world? They live too deep in the jungle to be easily accessible. They are way too wild and erratic to approach. They are way too heavy to airlift by helicopter. How do they capture elephants? The answer to this question is quite fascinating.

The captors first tranquilize the elephant with a dart. While the animal is asleep, they tie its leg to a tree. The elephant wakes up weak and groggy, tries to move only to find itself bound to the tree. It tries again, and fails. After a couple of days of trying unsuccessfully to move, the elephant finally gives up. It arrives at the sad but incorrect conclusion that as long as the chain is tied to its leg, it cannot escape. Once the elephant reaches this semi-catatonic state, the captors loose the chain from the tree, and they walk the elephant into captivity, while the animal tamely acquiesces.

If at any point the elephant could only realize that it is now free, it would rise up on its hind legs, make the elephant noise, and escape. But alas, the elephant is no longer bound by the chain, it is now bound by incorrect beliefs.

This is what strongholds do to us. Even though Christ has set us free, our thoughts and imaginations keep us in bondage. Do you feel as though you are in bondage to sin, or in bondage to trials? Do you feel as though you are in bondage to the devil, such that anything the devil does is guaranteed to succeed? Do you feel you cannot live for God because the devil has you bound? Do you think you cannot stop sinning because Satan keeps making you sin?

Then you feel so condemned that you cannot even stand before God to pray with a clear conscience. Perhaps, like the elephant, you stopped trying to pray. Chances are you are not bound by the devil at all. Chances are that you are bound by your own thoughts, and you blame the devil for it.

The devil made me do it

Have you ever heard a Christian say, *"The devil made me do it. Look what the devil made me do"?* Perhaps you can identify a sin you keep falling into over and over again. Perhaps you can identify an area where the devil keeps tempting you and you just can't seem to kick it. People often think that they sin because the devil tempted them. Sure the devil tempts, that is his job. But the only reason temptations take root is because of strongholds in our minds.

You try to bind the devil, rebuke the temptation, or scramble for some scripture to quote. Maybe you try to will yourself to resist the temptation. But it does not work. Nothing works. That's because you misunderstand how temptations work. You are aiming your big guns at the devil, when you should be redirecting your weapons of war at the strongholds in your own mind. The devil is not as big as you think. He is small, but he is smart. He is like the elephant captor. He cannot overpower the elephant, so he gets the elephant to capture himself. Similarly, the devil is no match for a child of God, but he works through weaknesses in our own flesh and mind to fight against us.

It is a myth to believe that the devil can make you do anything you don't want to do. As we discussed in Chapter 7, Christians cannot be demonized or demon possessed, therefore we are never under the control of the enemy. It is true that the devil can send temptations, but that is not sufficient to make us sin. In every temptation, God provides a way of escape *(1 Corinthians 10:13)*. James says we sin when we are drawn away by our own lusts *(James 1:14)*. This is why Jesus taught us to pray for God to lead us away from temptation. God is the one in control, not the devil.

The reason we sin is not because the devil tempted us or the devil made us do it. We sin because we have something that the devil can work with.

Another preacher put it much more succinctly – we sin because we like it. We sin because we have strongholds that give root to Satan's temptation. In order for us to resist temptation, we must first pull down the strongholds.

If there is a juicy mouth-watering chocolate cake in the refrigerator, you can will yourself to not eat it. But in the middle of the night when you wake up hungry, that hunger erodes any resistance your will can pose. The key is not strengthening your will-power, but finding a healthier alternative to satisfy your hunger. If you are not hungry, you won't eat the cake. Similarly, get rid of the strongholds, and the temptations lose their power.

What exactly are strongholds?

In the Old Testament, Israel fought against various enemies. The battle of Jericho was particularly interesting, because the people of Jericho had a huge wall around their city. This wall was a stronghold. It gave them a military advantage over any would-be attacker. The wall provided a major obstacle to the enemy, while giving the people of Jericho advance notice and time to prepare their defense. In order for Israel to siege Jericho, their real battle was against the wall. Once the stronghold came down, victory quickly followed.

The Bible also speaks of towers and mountains which provided the advantage of elevation. The higher you are, the better your chances of winning a war. This is why the psalmist referred to God as a strong tower or high tower (*Psalm 144:2; Proverbs 18:10*). These were physical objects that provided a military advantage, thus they were called strongholds.

The same idea carries over in the New Testament. Compare the following scriptures:

> *...we do not wrestle against flesh and blood, but against principalities, against powers .... (Ephesians 6:12)*
>
> *(For the weapons of our warfare are not carnal, but mighty through God to the pulling down of <u>strong holds</u>;) Casting down <u>imaginations</u>, and every high thing that exalteth itself against the <u>knowledge of God</u>, and bringing into captivity every <u>thought</u> to the obedience of Christ... (2 Corinthians 10:4-5, KJV, emphasis mine)*

We can see that spiritual strongholds are clearly identified with thoughts and imaginations. They are patterns of thinking that are contrary to the Word of God. Similar to Old Testament strongholds, these strongholds in our minds give the devil a strategic advantage over us. This is the reason why his temptations work over and over again.

We are fighting against the devil's kingdom, but we are not fighting him directly. That's the mistake we make too often. We often focus on engaging the enemy in combat when the real battle is against the stronghold. Our weapons are not for pulling down principalities and powers, but rather for the pulling down of strongholds. Once we get rid of the stronghold, the devil has nothing to work with, and the temptations cannot take root. In other words, <u>we wrestle against the devil's kingdom by using our weapons of warfare to attack the strongholds in our minds</u>.

<u>Lions go after the weakest prey</u>

The devil is portrayed as a roaring lion seeking whom he may devour. A lion does not look for a fight just to prove that he is the king of the jungle. There are many animals that lions generally do not mess with. They don't mess with elephants, hippos, rhinos and crocodiles. They don't pick battles they are likely to lose. They go after cattle and buffalo, and not just that, they go after the little ones who might be walking with a limp or separate from the herd. They go after the weakest prey. The devil goes after our weaknesses.

Temptations themselves have no real power. The only thing that gives them power is our flesh – our sinful nature. The Bible uses many different words and expressions to describe this sinful nature – flesh, carnal mind, old man, body of death, lust of the flesh.

> *... put on the new man, which after God is created in righteousness and true holiness ... (Ephesians 4:24)*

> *For the desires of the flesh are against the Spirit, and the desires of the Spirit are against the flesh; for these are opposed to each other, to prevent you from doing what you would ... (Galatians 5:17, RSV)*

> *For I delight in the law of God according to the inward man. But I see another law in my members, warring against the law of my mind, and bringing me into captivity to the law of sin which is in my members ... (Romans 7:22-23)*

Children of God are created in true holiness and righteousness, but we still have the old sinful nature to contend with. So we have two natures at work in us. The new regenerated nature wishes to follow after God and live righteously. But the sinful nature fights against it. We want to live right, but our sinful nature keeps resisting us. This is the stronghold that keeps us in bondage to sin.

Pulling down strongholds

Paul told us that if we walk in the Spirit, we will not fulfill the lust of the flesh (*Galatians 5:16*). So the key to overcoming temptation is walking in the Spirit as opposed to the flesh. The key is not binding the devil, but having the mind of Christ as opposed to the carnal mind. The key is pulling down the strongholds that are in our carnal mind and renewing our mind.

Many Christians would like to believe their problems can all be solved by having someone lay hands on them and providing deliverance. Unfortunately, there is no demon that we need deliverance from. What we need deliverance from is wrong patterns of thinking. We need to crucify the flesh. We cannot cast out the flesh. Deliverance is a one-and-done deal. Once the demon is cast out, he is out and the person is restored to normal. Crucifying the flesh on the other hand is a lifelong battle that requires daily death and self-denial. It is not easy.

Jesus was tempted by the devil, and as we know, each time he used the Word of God to resist the devil – *"it is written"*. However, it is a mistake to think that simply quoting scripture is the key to resisting the devil. Jesus did more than just quote the Word. He was the Word. Jesus had no sinful nature as we do, therefore the temptations had no chance of taking root. If we want to overcome temptations, we need to do much more than quote the Word. We need to have the Word of God ingrained in us. The Bible says that the engrafted word will save our souls.

In the next chapter, we will look at how three members of our *Bible Issues* Facebook group used the Word of God to destroy strongholds in their own lives.

CHAPTER 12

TESTIMONIES OF PULLING DOWN STRONGHOLDS

In the last chapter we talked about how the devil uses strongholds in our minds to keep us in bondage. We need to direct our weapons of war at destroying those strongholds by renewing our minds. I am pretty sure you have heard that teaching before. The unanswered question in many Christians' minds is how exactly do we use the Word of God to pull down strongholds?

I have interviewed three members of our *Bible Issues* Facebook group, and I have presented their testimonies of how they were able to pull down various strongholds in their lives. All of their names have been changed for privacy purposes. Be blessed by their stories.

How Jenna forgave her absent father

Jenna was 4 years old when her dad walked out on them, leaving behind a stay-at-home mom and two young children. He did not even tell them he was leaving. He just never came home from work one day. It took them quite a while to figure out that he had in fact left to be with somebody else. Although Jenna has no memory of it, her mother told her that she cried every day for weeks because she missed her daddy. The entire family had such a beautiful future, but that was all taken away from Jenna that day.

Jenna's father was a successful attorney with his own law firm, but there were no alimony payments forthcoming. That threw their entire world into a tailspin. Her mom had to scramble to find a job. They could not afford the apartment they were living in. During that first year, they changed apartments three times because they kept falling short of being able to afford the rent. Jenna has one haunting memory of her mom sobbing silently after she had lost an apartment because she could not afford the deposit. She reached out her 4-year old hand to comfort her mom. For whatever it was worth, she was there for her mom.

Jenna's family ended up living in a room in her grandparents' house. She had to continually drown out the noise of her mom being cursed out by her grandfather who never liked them. Jenna was entrusted to various babysitters – one of them being an uncle who turned out to be a pedophile.

Little by little Jenna's mom was able to build her own house whenever she saved some money. Because of how unbearable their living arrangement had become, they decided to move into the house before they could even afford to put up windows and install running water. Many nights, her mom slept by the door because a drug-addicted neighbor was threatening to rape her two daughters.

This was Jenna's childhood. She grew up in poverty even though her father was a successful attorney who lived in a 3-storey mansion. Unfortunately none of that money trickled down to her, since her stepmother did not want her husband's *"illegitimate"* children to interfere with her new life.

One day, Jenna and her sister saw their dad in the mall, and they ran up to him and kissed him. Her stepmother promptly took them aside and warned them to never do that again since it would *"destroy her dad's image"*. Jenna never kissed her father again for two decades. These experiences hardened her and she grew up tough. She forgot how to cry as the love of a father was cruelly stolen from her. Imagine the effect that this image of a father would have on Jenna's image of a heavenly Father.

At age 18, Jenna enrolled in medical school. Even though she grew up poor and her mom had nothing but a high school education, she pounded into Jenna and her sister's heads that they would go to university, get good jobs and be independent so they would never have to depend on a man financially. With the help of two scholarships, Jenna was able to navigate medical school.

Revenge was Jenna's main motivation. She was determined that once she got her big job, she would walk over to her father's firm, tell him what she thought of him in very colorful language, and let him know that she succeeded in spite of him. However, God would interrupt Jenna's plans.

Jenna came to know Jesus as her personal Lord and Savior at age 19. Amazingly her father who was steeped in another religion, suddenly showed up and tried to steer her away from the Christian God. Nevertheless, her faith prevailed. Soon God began to minister to her that she needed to forgive her father and stepmother. She knew that unless and until she dealt with the anger and resentment against her own dad, it would be difficult for her to relate to God as Father, and also to relate to a future husband. So she was determined to forgive.

She printed out as many scriptures as she could find on fathers, forgiveness, mercy and God's love. She began to meditate on those verses over and over. She continually read them, and some of them she committed to memory. Whenever she had some time to spare, she would pull those scriptures out of her purse and read. If she was in a waiting room, or waiting for a class, she would read those verses. Sometimes she would read them over 50 times in a day. One of her favorite verses was,

> *A father of the fatherless, a defender of widows, Is God in His holy habitation ... (Psalm 68:5)*

This went on for three years. During this time, Jenna also spent a lot of time in prayer and surrender to God – crying out to Him and asking Him to take the resentment and bitterness out of her heart. She laid herself bare before God. All of her hurt and pain, she gave it to God. Having not been able to cry for years due to continual hardening, she found herself crying uncontrollably during her prayer time.

Personally she found this easier to do alone than in a corporate group. But she did have prayer partners who also had issues they were working through. They shared their pains, prayed for one another, and they were able to help each other through.

When Jenna was finished with her medical degree and landed her first job, the time had come to confront her father and let him know exactly what she thought of him. But by then, God had removed the sword from her heart. There was no longer any desire for payback. During her intense prayer time, she was able to forgive her father from her heart (*Matthew 18:35*).

At this point she called her dad and verbally expressed her forgiveness for all he did and did not do. She felt the anger leave. During her prayer and meditation, she had seen a gradual and consistent improvement. That brought her to a place where she could have finally made this call. This was when the dramatic change took place.

Her friends saw it. She was no longer an emotional wreck suffering from inexplicable mood swings. She was no longer angry and resentful. She had learned that God forgave her of her sins when she did not deserve to be forgiven, and with that mercy in her, she was able to forgive her unforgiveable father. If you saw Jenna today, you would never know that she was an abandoned child from a broken home. You would never know. Such is the healing power that Jenna experienced through forgiveness.

How JR pulled down a stronghold of lust

JR's father was a *"player"*, who slept around. He saw the effect it had on his mother. He was also aware that this gene might be in him. He did not want to grow up like his father. Nevertheless JR had a problem with lust throughout his teenage years and into his early thirties. He was addicted to porn and struggled with impure thoughts that left him feeling condemned.

Like many other Christians, JR made the mistake of thinking that getting married would solve this problem. It did not. Even after he was married, he found himself lusting after women other than his wife. That made him very uncomfortable because he desperately did not want to be like his own father. He hated himself for it, but did not know how to stop those thoughts.

By the grace of God, he never acted on those thoughts. He never cheated on his wife. But it was still affecting his marriage. As a born-again Christian, he did not want to be thinking sexually about women other than his wife.

Sometime in his early 30s, JR made a decision that he was going to be free from this bondage. But he recognized that it was not as simple as deciding to stop thinking those thoughts. Only God could truly make this change. Although it was difficult, he knew it was possible.

JR noticed something that gave him hope. Lust acted up mainly when he was alone. If there were other people around e.g. his pastor, he did not have the lustful thoughts. So that gave him hope – he knew he could learn to control those thoughts even when his pastor was not around. He believed that he could trust in God for help when something seemed impossible. JR was convicted by scriptures like,

> *Your Word have I hidden in my heart that I might not sin against You ... (Psalm 119:11)*

> *...whatever things are true ... noble ... just ... pure ... lovely ... meditate on these things ... (Philippians 4:8)*

> *But his delight is in the law of the Lord, and in His law he meditates day and night... (Psalm 1:2)*

So he decided he was going to use the Word to destroy that stronghold. Unlike Jenna, JR did not see the point in using a handful of scriptures directly dealing with lust and thoughts. He believed he needed the entire Word of God. He was not sure how to meditate on a scripture, so he just started studying the Word. He did not limit himself to any specific portion of the Bible. He focused, not on memorizing or repeating the verses over and over, but on the message that was contained in the scripture – the whole Bible. He would pray, and wherever the Spirit led him, those are the portions of scripture he would use on any given day.

From the book of Galatians, JR knew he could either walk in the Spirit or the flesh. He could either operate in the carnal mind or the mind of Christ. He pictured his mind as a narrow door through which only one person could fit. If someone is going out, no one else could come in at the same time. Similarly, the narrow door of his mind could either entertain God's Word or evil thoughts – not both at the same time. So JR used the Word of God to accomplish a two-fold effect.

1) The act of studying the Word had a gradual renewing of his mind.
2) The Word of God also acted as a distraction that kept impure thoughts out. As long as the Word was occupying the doorway, no impure thought could pass through.

During times when he felt the temptations coming on strong, he would deliberately distract himself by thinking about the Word, listening to some worship music, or playing with his kids – anything other than feeding those thoughts. This was his way of fleeing youthful lusts.

Did JR have to spend the rest of his life distracting himself from impure thoughts – because that sure sounds like bondage? The answer is no. According to him, over time, the lustful thoughts gradually lost their hold on his mind. Today (*he is in his mid-30s*), those thoughts no longer have the controlling effect that they once did. It does get better, once you weather the storm. Temptations are for a season, and once you endure, the devil leaves.

> *And when the devil had ended all the temptation, he departed from him for a season ... (Luke 4:13)*
>
> *Resist the devil and he will flee from you ... (James 4:7)*

How Madison overcame the fear of public speaking

Madison was an introverted lawyer. Early in her legal career, she had a serious problem with fear and lack of self-confidence. During meetings she would be a nervous wreck, paralyzed to speak. It would take her quite a while to muster the courage to finally say something – after everyone else had already moved on to the next point. Could you imagine a lawyer who was afraid of speaking? That was Madison.

She realized that she simply could not continue like that if she were to be a successful attorney. So she printed out all the scriptures that talked about fear and courage. She read and studied a book by Neil Anderson called *Living Free in Christ*. She essentially gave herself a crash course on overcoming fear because her career as a negotiator depended on it. She did this day and night until she got these fear scriptures ingrained in her mind and heart. Her favorite was,

> *For God has not given us a spirit of fear, but of power and of love and of a sound mind ... (2 Timothy 1:7)*

She realized that this was not a demon spirit of fear, but a stronghold of fear that needed to come down. Sometimes, she wished it were a demon, because then she could cast it out and move on with her life. But renewing the mind took work and time. She also learned that fear is rooted in not realizing how big God is. She started to meditate on scriptures that spoke of God's bigness.

> *If God is for us, who can be against us? ... (Romans 8:31)*

She reasoned that if she could go boldly to the very throne of God Almighty in times of need, why should she be afraid of speaking to or in the presence of any human being? She learned to magnify God in her eyes, and she learned who she is in Christ.

Gradually, she was able to conquer that fear of speaking. The change was most noticeable one day when she found herself joking with foreign diplomats who were meeting with her company. Her friends looked at her in astonishment, because that was completely against her character to be that bold and confident. Through meditating on God's Word and learning to see how big her God is, Madison was able to transform her very personality.

Madison has now spoken in front of royalty, presidents, parliamentarians, senators, judges, and CEOs. She has never had a problem with fear since. Madison learned how to revel in the bigness of her God.

How should we pray?

We have seen three examples of individuals who used the Word of God to destroy strongholds, renew their minds and to get deliverance from bondage. Notice that none of them blamed the devil for their problems.

Perhaps you are wondering how you can destroy the strongholds in your own life and gain freedom from bondage.

1) Identify the sin that easily besets you. What is the sin or problem that makes you stumble every time? That's the area of your flesh that is prone to the devil. That is your stronghold.
2) Get the scriptures that apply. Don't just look for scriptures on fear, lust or forgiveness. Are there other underlying issues? Get scriptures on those as well.
3) Read those scriptures over and over. Meditate on them. Study them. Talk to other Christians about them.
4) As you study them prayerfully, allow them to change your very thinking. Ask God to teach you how to operate in the mind of Christ. We already have God's mind in us, we just need to learn how to get our own mind out of the way.
5) When temptations arise that want you to go back to your old ways, get out your scriptures, sing some worship songs, or find some way of distracting yourself. Don't feed the temptations, so that way the devil will get no traction.
6) Pray, fast and ask for God's help. Through faith, you can move any mountain.

As you continue the process, God may show you other issues that you need to address. This process is often like an onion – existing in layers – where you only discover deeper issues after you peel through the outer layers. Be open to His leading and guidance. I pray that God will deliver you from the bondage associated with the flesh and the mind, and help you to remove the strongholds so that you can truly live free in Christ.

MYTH #7

GOD IS ANGRY WITH ME

How this myth keeps us in bondage

This myth reduces God to a vindictive ogre who is not just small, but small minded. It very subtly believes in a God who is simply not worth praying to. How could our prayers possibly be effective if we see God this way? This myth also believes in a God who is always angry with us and punishes us with demons whenever we sin. It is based on a gross misunderstanding of the very atonement of Christ.

What you will learn in the next two chapters

- God is defined as being merciful and slow to anger
- God does not punish, He chastens
- We do not become *"fair game"* to the devil when we sin
- We can be confident in the security we have in Christ

Let the truth free you from the burden of believing that God is angry with you and waiting to punish you every chance He gets. Let the truth free you from the burden of believing that you have to be scared of the devil every time you fall short.

CHAPTER 13

DO WE SERVE AN ANGRY GOD?

I punished you because you did not pray

An acquaintance of mine was recently a victim of a robbery. He was taking his teenaged daughter to school when they were blocked off by another vehicle. A passenger from the other vehicle came out with a gun and ordered the man and his daughter out of the car. The bandits proceeded to drive away with both cars. Fortunately for my acquaintance, the vehicle was fully insured. Even more fortunately, both he and his daughter were unharmed.

How do you think you would feel if you were in their shoes? I can tell from personal experience that surviving a trauma fills you with awe of God's mercy and goodness. On July 31, 2009, I was also car-jacked and abducted at gunpoint by three armed men. Their primary interest was the car, but they needed me out of the way so they could get away before I called the police. So they took my phone and gently (?) placed me in the trunk of the car. They actually hit me with the gun and threw me in. I still have the mark on my forehead as a reminder.

For 30 minutes in that trunk with blood literally gushing out of my head, I prayed like I never prayed before. I cried out to God, I confessed every sin, I prayed for everyone that I had wronged. I let the devil know who was in control. I prayed for God to somehow preserve my life, but in the worst-case scenario, to take me home and to take care of my family.

Then my abductors stopped near an abandoned oil field, took me out and tied me up on the ground. One of them was pointing the gun to my head, while the others in the background were prodding him, *"Kill him, shoot him"*. I vowed to myself that I was not going to cry or beg for my life. I simply prayed silently, *"Lord my life is in Your hands, not theirs, not the devil's. They can do nothing that you do not allow them to do. You are God."*

Well they obviously did not kill me. They drove off with the car and I was able to loose myself and find help. Three days later, we recovered the car fully intact with the keys in the ignition. All I lost materially was $300 that was in my wallet. For everything and in everything, I was extremely thankful to God for His mercy and goodness, which I did not consider myself to have deserved. Around the same time, another guy went missing, and they found his body two days later with a gunshot wound to his head. That could have been me. I was just thankful for God's mercy.

Many of my friends visited me when they heard what had happened. I remember my pastor praying that God would help me to forgive my attackers. I thought about how much wisdom was embedded in that prayer, because it was so easy for someone in my position to be resentful or bitter. But I actually felt no resentment whatsoever toward them, such that I didn't even think I had anything to forgive them for. I never felt like a victim because I was supposed to be dead, but instead God spared my life. If anything, I thank God for them that they did not kill me.

Back to the earlier story. My acquaintance narrated his story afterward, and thanked God for preserving his and his daughter's lives. Then he said something that got me thinking. Normally on mornings they prayed together before they left home. But on this day, they were so busy that all they could muster was a quick prayer on the road. He said that God later spoke to him and told him that the reason they got robbed was because they did not pray properly that morning. However the quick prayer that they did pray was what saved their lives during the robbery.

Immediately I recognized that God did not tell him that. This was just his mind, held in bondage by God-limiting myths, playing tricks on him. This was his own thoughts and ideas, and he called it God. Trust me, it happens all the time. He thought the God he served was so vindictive, that He would send criminals to rob and traumatize them just because they did not pray properly.

Now if they were in the habit of not praying at all, that was a different story. God occasionally uses trials to jolt us back to where we need to be. But that was not the case with them. They prayed every morning. Essentially in his mind, God was prepared to kill his family because they were too busy to pray one day. Wow, his god is not just small, he is small-minded. Thank God I don't serve that god.

God is slow to anger

This guy's understanding of God is flawed. The God of the Bible is merciful and slow to anger. Yes He does get angry sometimes, but He is not vindictive against His own children.

> *His anger is but for a moment, His favor is for a lifetime ... (Psalm 30:5, NASB)*

Moses saw God's glory and the first thing he noticed was God's mercy and grace. I bet this is not what comes to mind when you think of God's glory.

> *And he said, "Please, show me Your glory."*
>
> *And the Lord passed before him and proclaimed, "The Lord, the Lord God, merciful and gracious, longsuffering, and abounding in goodness and truth, keeping mercy for thousands, forgiving iniquity and transgression and sin, by no means clearing the guilty, visiting the iniquity of the fathers upon the children and the children's children to the third and the fourth generation."*
>
> *... Exodus 33:18; 34:6-7, emphasis mine*

I know from experience, that when you survive any kind of trauma, you are normally so in awe of God's mercy and goodness. I have been there, and I cannot understand how someone who just experienced the mercy and goodness of God, could paint such a spiteful picture of God. That is called bondage, and it is caused by God-limiting myths.

Chastening vs. punishment

Before we got saved, most of us had the image of God holding a stick over us to punish us whenever we sin. Here is the thing. Sin was punished on Calvary. That's why Jesus came to this earth and died such a horrific death on the cross. He did that to pay the penalty for sin. Every sin we ever committed and every sin we will ever commit were all paid for on that cross. God will never punish us for sin. That is a myth based on a misunderstanding of God and a misunderstanding of Christ's atonement.

God does not punish, He chastens. The difference is huge. Chastening is something that comes out of God's love for us. God does not chasten us because we sin, but because He wants us to partake of His holiness and righteousness.

> *For whom the Lord loves He chastens ... that we may be partakers of His holiness ... (Hebrews 12:6,10)*

Here is a simple example that illustrates the difference. I know a parent who would punish her son by banning him from church. As a child, the son wanted to go to church, so his mother figured, what better way to punish him than to take away something he liked. *"No church for you!"* What a foolish parent! Instead of punishing, she should have chastened. Take away a toy that he liked and make him give it to a less privileged child. That would be chastening. It involves a degree of punishment, but it also teaches invaluable lessons.

In addition, sin may have consequences. When David sinned with Bathsheba, God killed the child that was born, and He vowed that the sword would never leave David's house. The reason for this is clearly spelled out in scripture – David had given the enemies of God an occasion to blaspheme *(2 Samuel 12:14)*. So some sins – especially if they are public sins – have consequences. If you commit adultery, God will forgive you, but there is no guarantee your husband or wife will. There is no guarantee that the relationship will ever recover.

It is finished!

Make no mistake, sin is horrible. Sin is ugly. But Jesus already dealt with sin on the cross. Many of us feel we have to pay for our sins. This is a myth that puts you in bondage. Then whenever you commit sin, you feel condemned and you are afraid to even go to God in prayer. You try to hide from God like Adam. You are so much in bondage that you cannot even pray. If only you understood how merciful God is.

> *For we do not have a High Priest who cannot sympathize with our weaknesses, but was in all points tempted as we are, yet without sin. Let us therefore come boldly to the throne of grace, that we may obtain mercy and find grace to help in time of need ... (Hebrews 4:15-16)*

We are commanded to go boldly to God in prayer. The time of need in this verse is when we are under heavy temptation and we are feeling weak, and perhaps already fallen into sin. Instead of cowering from God in fear, go boldly to God for mercy and grace. God gives us grace and strength *(2 Corinthians 12:9)* and does not condemn us *(Romans 8:1)*.

Rid your mind of this God-distorting myth that God is a vindictive ogre ready to beat up on us whenever we sin. We have a high priest who can empathize with our infirmity. He was tempted in every way yet without sin. So when we sin, He comforts us and says *"Hey, I already paid for your sin. Let Satan accuse and condemn all he wants, I prayed for you. You are forgiven."* Jesus would leave the 99 sheep to go after the one that went astray. He is the Good Shepherd. Our loving heavenly Father is looking out for us whenever we fall, waiting for us to come back. In fact, His goodness is leading us back to repentance *(Romans 2:4)*. God is not small-minded. He is not vindictive.

How would you handle freedom?

Suppose your boss recognizes that you are very stressed out at work and your productivity is suffering. He looks into the matter, and realizes that the traffic on your daily commute is the main culprit. As an experiment, he gives you the option of working from home 2 days a week. He is obviously testing to see what effect this will have on your productivity.

What would you do if you were afforded that opportunity? Would you loaf and go to the beach during your two days off? Or would you work extra hard to make sure your productivity does not decrease so you won't lose this wonderful privilege? I think if you were smart enough to purchase this book, you would probably choose the latter.

That is how God works with us. He places us in the position of security and gives us the freedom to serve Him. He does not stand over us with a stick like these old-fashioned bosses. I have seen foremen on construction sites speaking down to their employees, belittling them and calling them racist epithets. I have even seen pastors who talk down to their followers. That is not how God treats us. Rid your mind of this God-distorting myth of a small-minded vindictive God. That is not the God of the Bible.

Sinners in the hands of an angry God?

There is a popular sermon by Jonathan Edwards called *Sinners in the hands of an angry God*. This sermon has been lauded by more preachers than I care to remember. Here is an excerpt from it.

> *If you cry to God to pity you, he will be so far from pitying you ... He will not only hate you, but he will have you in the utmost Contempt; no place shall be thought fit for you, but under his Feet, to be trodden down as the Mire of the Streets.* [12]

I can't believe he actually said that God will hate you. This has to be one of the most unscriptural sermons I have ever heard. With all due respect to Jonathan Edwards, I will preach about the mercy of God. If people choose to take advantage of God's mercy, that is up to them. But I will not attempt to frighten people into serving God. God wants us to have a reverential fear of Him, not to be afraid of Him.

Don't distort God's image

There are variations of this particular myth, as we will see in the next chapter. But whatever the specific form, it involves a misunderstanding or limiting of Christ's atonement. We make our sins big and Christ's atonement small. We distort the image of God from a merciful Father to a vindictive angry beast. In the next chapter, we will look at some other similar myths and how they keep you in bondage.

CHAPTER 14

DOES SIN GIVE THE DEVIL ACCESS TO US?

The previous chapter introduced a myth that reduces God to an angry ogre, and neglects His great mercy toward us. This chapter exposes a number of myths that also neglect the mercy and grace of God – myths that minimize the great work that Jesus did on the cross when He gave His life for our sins.

Does sin open portals to demons?

I read a book recently where the author claims that sin (*especially sexual sin*) opens *portals to demons.*[13] Right off the bat, I am going to tell you that is a myth. It is simply not true. That did not come from the Bible.

The very fact that the author uses the word *"portal"* says a lot. That word *"portal"* does not appear in <u>any</u> English translation of the Bible. On the contrary, *"portal"* shows up a lot in the occult. That word alone suggests that this teaching did not come from the Bible but from some witch movie.

Secondly, this myth acts as though demons are independent entities who act in response to spiritual laws. They are not. They act in accordance with God's will. God is big and demons are small. But this myth makes demons bigger than they really are. This myth causes us to believe that if we sin, oops, we just opened the portal and demons now have access to us.

Look at these three scriptures:

> *Simon, Simon! Indeed, Satan has asked for you, that he may sift you as wheat. <u>But I have prayed for you</u>... (Luke 22:31-32, emphasis mine)*

> *...if anyone sins, we have an Advocate with the Father, Jesus Christ the righteous ... (1 John 2:1)*

> *...where sin abounded, grace abounded much more ... (Romans 5:20)*

If sin opened doors to demons, the people who wrote the Bible did not seem to know about it. These verses hardly paint a picture of demons gaining access to us when we sin. Ideally we should not sin. But if and when we sin, that's when we truly experience God's grace. When we sin, our defense lawyer stands in the gap and says, *"I have prayed for them"*. The Bible does not teach that Christians become fair game to the devil when they sin. I challenge you to find one verse of scripture that teaches this.

Demons act in accordance with God's will. Demons only have access to us if God permits it. The devil could not get anywhere near Job because of God's hedge around him. It was only when God gave the devil limited access that he was finally able to buffet Job. But you may ask, *"I am not as righteous as Job, does this apply to me?"* You are actually more righteous that Job. Job was not sinless, but if you are a born-again child of God, you are the very righteousness of the sinless Son of God (*2 Corinthians 5:21*). Of course you are protected in Christ.

Now do not get the wrong impression. I am not trying to teach you how to sin and get away with it. That would be an entirely different myth. What I am trying to do is show you the scriptural truth so you can walk in freedom. I trust that if you really love God, you will not attempt to take advantage of His grace.

Can other people's demons be transferred to me?

Another author expanded on the myth that sin opens portals to demons. He warned that unsaved people can have demons in their lives, and we may not know about it. Then when we go to the salon to do our hair or nails, their demons can get inadvertently transferred to us without us knowing.[14]

According to this myth, Christians get opened up to demons even when we don't sin. Sometimes you have to wonder if there is a school out there called *Christian Mythology for Dummies* that these people graduated from. They insist on limiting God. They somehow cannot accept the idea that God is large and in charge.

There is not one verse of scripture that says other people's demons can be transferred to Christians. We have already established that demons cannot possess Christians. Why would demons leave an established home to try to move somewhere that is uninhabitable to them? There was an incident where someone was possessed by demons, and some non-Christians were trying to cast it out. Here is what happened.

> *Then some of the itinerant Jewish exorcists took it upon themselves to call the name of the Lord Jesus over those who had evil spirits, saying, "We exorcise you by the Jesus whom Paul preaches."*

And the evil spirit answered and said, "Jesus I know, and Paul I know; but who are you?" Then the man in whom the evil spirit was leaped on them, overpowered them, and prevailed against them, so that they fled out of that house naked and wounded

... Acts 19:13-16

The Bible tells us that the demon-possessed man beat up those non-Christian exorcists and sent them running away naked. But it did not say that the demons were transferred to them. So even in this case, the idea of demons being transferred to unsaved people was not taught in scripture. Why would you think demons could be inadvertently transferred to Christians? Is your God really that small? If I am a Christian, and a demon could be transferred to me, then that demon is bigger than the God who lives in me. On the contrary, the Bible teaches that the greater One lives in me than that any demon in the world.

Is it so hard for Christians to go to heaven?

I once heard a Christian lament, *"It is so hard for Christians to go to heaven."* Everyone looked at her as if she was mad. She continued, *"All it takes is one sin, and you could miss heaven."* So I simply posed the question to her, *"Why exactly did Jesus die then?"*

This is so sad. This is the ultimate bondage. This person was a nervous wreck living every waking minute thinking she could miss heaven, and trying to maintain her salvation by living a good life. It is sad.

Have you ever looked at the end of a close basketball match? One team scores and takes the lead. Then the other team scores, now they have the lead. Back and forth it goes. So it comes down to which team has the last possession. It comes down to which team could hold their nerve to better negotiate the clock. It's nerve wrecking.

This person was a nervous wreck thinking her salvation was a matter of beating the buzzer. If she sins before she dies, she goes to hell. But if she dies before she sins, she makes it to heaven. Phew! That is called bondage. Read the following scriptures:

... who are <u>kept by the power of God</u> through faith unto salvation ... (1 Peter 1:5, emphasis mine)

But the Lord is faithful, who shall stablish you, and <u>keep you from evil</u> ... (2 Thessalonians 3:3, emphasis mine)

> Now unto him that is able to <u>keep you from falling</u>, and to <u>present you faultless</u> before the presence of his glory with exceeding joy ... (Jude 24, emphasis mine)

> ...the Spirit Himself makes intercession for us... (Romans 8:26-27)

> Therefore He is also able to save to the uttermost those who come to God through Him, since He always lives to make intercession for them ... (Hebrews 7:25)

These scriptures all teach that if you are in Christ, God is preserving and keeping you. Both Jesus and the Holy Spirit are interceding for us. Note that I am not preaching easy-believism. We do have a responsibility to remain in Christ.

> ...let us hold fast our confession... (Hebrews 4:14)

> ...continue in the grace of God ... (Acts 13:43)

> ...continue in the faith... (Acts 14:22)

Theologians will debate until the end of time whether or not Christians can lose their salvation. Some of them will even continue the debate in heaven. This is outside the scope of this book, but here is something over which there is <u>no</u> debate. No Christian should ever live in <u>fear</u> of inadvertently losing their salvation. We often quote the following scripture:

> Love has been perfected among us in this: that we may have <u>boldness in the day of judgment</u> .... There is no fear in love; but <u>perfect love casts out fear</u> ... But he who fears has not been made perfect in love ... (1 John 4:17-18, emphasis mine)

What fear do you think that is referring to? Fear of spiders? Fear of the dark? If we are afraid of snakes, does that mean God's love is not perfected in us? This verse is talking about the fear of losing your salvation. How do I know this? It's because the opposite of fear *(in this context)* is boldness on the Day of Judgment. Since it is speaking about a specific kind of boldness, it must also be speaking about a specific kind of fear. The opposite of boldness on judgment day is fear of losing your salvation.

If we really understood the full extent of God's love that Jesus demonstrated on Calvary, we would never be timid before the throne of God, but bold. If we understood who we are in Christ, we would never live in the tormenting fear of losing our salvation. We should be confident in God's preserving power, and never afraid of losing our salvation.

If you are afraid of losing your salvation, it's because of God-distorting myths that keep you in bondage. God is big even when it comes to your eternal salvation. He started the work in you, and He has promised to complete it. It is all by His grace.

Is God punishing me because I am rebellious?

A believer in Christ made a decision to leave the church he was in and find another church because of personal and doctrinal differences with the pastor. He felt the church had become too cultic. Not too long after this, he became ill. So the first thought that entered his mind was that God was punishing him for being rebellious.

He remembered other people who had also left churches, and bad things happened to them. One of them was *"stricken"* with Parkinson's and died. Another one eventually was murdered. All of these memories conspired to convince him that God was now punishing him with illness.

It turned out to only be food poisoning. The illness soon passed. And one day, unless the rapture takes place before, this person will die. It does not mean that God struck him down with death.

Again, this bondage is caused by misunderstanding how big the love of God is. We are God's children. If two of your kids had a disagreement, how would you handle it? Would you take sides and punish the bad one? No you won't. You are too smart for that. I mean you bought this book didn't you? You will try to resolve the problem and teach both sides a lesson. Your goal is to get both of them back into right standing.

God does not have favorites. I know it does not always feel that way, trust me, I know. He may have different purposes for each person. But we all tend to magnify our own trials and minimize other people's trials. You simply do not know what other people go through and how you would handle it if you had to carry their cross. You simply do not know.

Romans 11 gives us insight into how God resolves conflict. Israel was God's chosen people but they kept rebelling against Him. So in the fullness of time, God temporarily cast aside Israel and offered salvation to the Gentiles. Gentiles obtain mercy through Israel's disobedience *(Romans 11:31)*. But His goal is to provoke the Jews to jealousy so they can return to Him so that He might have mercy on all *(Romans 11:32)*. In the end, God would have saved both Jews and Gentiles.

This is how God resolves conflict. He does not pick sides. He does not punish one and bless the other. He may chasten if necessary. But He attempts to get all His children in good standing, and He will use the conflict to accomplish His purposes.

When you are being chastened, the temptation is to think that God is now cursing or punishing you, but the only reason you see it that way is because you have succumbed to myths that keep you in bondage. You may simply be going through a season of trials while the other person (*your foe*) may be going through a season of blessing. This could easily change in an instant, and even this does not indicate the favor of God. Blessings do not indicate God's favor, and chastening does not indicate His disfavor.

God's ways are above ours

I often wonder why some Christians believe in an angry God who punishes them with demons whenever they sin, and takes away their salvation every time they sneeze. The only reason I could think of is that they are projecting how things would have been if they were God. But that is precisely the point of Christianity – God is <u>not</u> like us. His ways are not our ways, His thought are not our thoughts. God's ways are above ours (*Isaiah 55:8-9*). His ways are past finding out (*Romans 11:33*). <u>Don't try to create god in your own image and likeness, because that god would only exist in your mind</u>. Our finite minds could never understand the love and grace of God.

See God the way the Bible portrays Him. He is not small and He is not small-minded. God is big. God is merciful and God is wise. If you are going through a trial, don't assume that it is because God hates you or is angry with you. God does get angry sometimes, but His anger only lasts a moment. His mercies are forever.

We all have our plans and aspirations in life. But we must also remember that God has His plans which are above ours. We don't know the full extent of God's plan for our lives, and we would not understand the full extent of His wisdom even if we knew His plan. He said that He cares for us (*1 Peter 5:7*) and that He loves us. Let us trust that God knows what He is doing.

We can assume that we have trials because God hates us, or we can assume we have trials because God loves us. One belief leads to bondage, the other one leads to liberty and peace. Let us put aside this myth that God is a vindictive angry God who loves to punish and hurt us. He is a loving, merciful God whose ways are past finding out. Rid your mind of these God-distorting myths, and let the truth of God's Word set you free.

MYTH #8

I NEED TO TAP INTO THAT GOD PRINCIPLE

How this myth keeps us in bondage

This myth reduces God to an impersonal force or principle that works with formulas. Because of this, it is constantly looking for new prayer formulas to move the hand of God, to receive blessings and to achieve prosperity. We thus follow new prayer trends rather than just pray the way the Bible taught us to pray, thus rendering our prayers ineffective.

What you will learn in the next two chapters

- There is no secret prayer formula
- God is not a principle, but a person
- God wants us to be persistent in prayer
- Prosperity only comes through following <u>all</u> the ingredients given in the Bible.

Let the truth free you from the burden of believing that you have to word your prayers correctly otherwise God would reject your prayers. Let the truth free you from the burden of giving away your money in ways God never intended to causes that God never endorsed.

CHAPTER 15

IS THERE A SECRET PRAYER FORMULA THAT MOVES GOD?

Finding the right prayer formula

I once heard a preacher use the following scripture to deliver a sermon on prayer.

> *Then He spoke a parable to them, that men always ought to <u>pray and not lose heart</u>, saying: "There was in a certain city a judge who did not fear God nor regard man.*
>
> *Now there was a widow in that city; and she came to him, saying, 'Get justice for me from my adversary.' And he would not for a while; but afterward he said within himself, 'Though I do not fear God nor regard man, yet because this widow troubles me I will avenge her, lest by her <u>continual coming</u> she weary me.'"*
>
> *Then the Lord said, "Hear what the unjust judge said. And shall God not avenge His own elect who cry out day and night to Him, though He bears long with them? I tell you that He will avenge them speedily. Nevertheless, when the Son of Man comes, <u>will He really find faith on the earth</u>?"*
>
> *... Luke 18:1-8, emphasis mine*

The preacher then gave his understanding of the passage.

> *I don't believe that God wants us to pray for the same thing over and over. He just wants us to pray for it once. Then afterward, we should focus on praising God for granting our request. Thank Him for the answer to our prayer.*
>
> *When you go to God over and over asking Him for the same thing, you are undoing your prayers. Prayer is like a seed. Every time you ask, you are digging up the ground and planting your seed over again. Every time you ask, you have to start the process over from scratch.*[15]

I sat there pulling the hair out of my head. Was this guy from another planet where they speak a language called *"hsilgnE"* – the opposite of English? Did he actually read the scripture? Seriously, if you wanted to preach that God does not want us to be persistent in prayer, then why would you use Luke 18? I was astonished. Even more astounding was the fact that everyone else was nodding in agreement and saying *"amen"*. Was I in the *Twilight Zone*?

I am pretty sure you have heard teachings like this. Perhaps you have actually tried using these techniques in your own prayer life. Instead of crying out to God and seeking Him diligently, your prayer life has become more regimented, more strategic. Instead of prayer being a means of relationship building with God, it is now more of a strategic plan to maximize your return on time invested in God.

God is not a principle

These kinds of teaching reduce God to an impersonal principle, and treat prayer as some kind of formula. Once you get the correct formula, the God-principle takes effect and your prayers get answered. If you apply the wrong formula, it does not work. These teachings are rampant because people are more interested in getting stuff from God than in a relationship with God Himself. What Christians don't realize is that these teachings are rooted in New Age non-Christian religions that believe in a god-force rather than a God Person. These teachings are an overlap where these New Age philosophies <u>appear</u> to intersect with Christianity.

I will show you in this chapter that you are supposed to be persistent in prayer. Contrary to the preacher above, God wants us to ask Him over and over for the same thing. There is no formula in prayer, instead prayer should be passionate and fervent. It should be heartfelt rather than strategic. I will demonstrate that God is not a principle that works with formulas, but a Father who seeks a relationship with His children. That is what our prayers should be about – building a personal relationship with God.

Christians who believe in the God-principle myth are constantly changing the way they pray. They keep jumping from one prayer strategy to the next until they find something that works. Plead the blood, rebuke the devil, bind and loose, name it and claim it, decree and declare. These are all prayer strategies that Christians have dabbled in over the past 30 years. They are grasping at anything that promises them some kind of answer. Oftentimes people tell me *"It really works, you should try it."*

Here is a question for you – how do you know it is the new prayer formula that worked? How do you know it was not someone else who prayed for you that God answered? Acts 17:30 tells us that in times of ignorance, God winked. It could be that God did not bless you <u>because of</u> your prayer, but <u>in spite</u> of your prayer. Instead of building a shrine for decree-and-declare and other make-shift doctrines, you should be thanking God for His grace and favor. It is God the person who blessed you, not the new prayer formula. You should be giving glory to God the person.

Instead of changing the way you pray every time you encounter a trial, you should be focused on examining your life to see if there are any hindrances to your prayers being answered. In Chapter 4, I listed quite a few of these hindrances that are mentioned in scripture.

God wants us to be persistent

The Luke 18 passage that I quoted earlier begins with the words, *"Then Jesus spoke a parable that men ought to pray always and not lose heart."* It ends with the words, *"When the son of man returns, will he find faith on earth?"* This means that persistence is a key ingredient in faith. Faith does not pray once. Faith prays without ceasing. Faith is relentless. Faith never gives up. Jesus gave this parable to teach that we ought to be persistent just like the woman in the parable.

But someone may object, *"God is not like that unjust judge."* Well I would hope not. Who ever said He was? Who said that unjust judge represented God? It is just a parable. The point of the parable was that as the woman was persistent enough to wear down an unjust judge, we should also be persistent in prayer. How much more favorably would our Heavenly Father, who is not unjust, respond to us? Jesus referred to this as faith.

This is similar to another parable Jesus gave, where a man came to his friend asking for bread. Even though he was not dealing with an unjust judge, he still had to be persistent.

> *...though he will not rise and give to him because he is his friend, yet <u>because of his persistence</u> he will rise and give him ... (Luke 11:8, emphasis mine)*

Again the message is that persistence caused the man's need to be met even though he was bothering his friend at the most inopportune time. Similarly, we should be persistent in prayer even though there is no inopportune time for God. Our God never sleeps. When the Bible says ask and you shall receive, it really meant ask and keep on asking, seek and keep on seeking, knock and keep on knocking.

There are numerous other scriptures that emphasize the point that we must persist. James spoke of the perseverance of Job (*James 5:11*). Paul taught us to pray always without ceasing (*1 Thessalonians 5:13*). Paul prayed for the same thing three times before God answered him (*2 Corinthians 12:8*). Even Jesus prayed for the same thing three times in the Garden of Gethsemane (*Matthew 26:44*). In the great faith chapter of the Bible, the author of Hebrews says that God is a rewarder of them that diligently seek him (*Hebrews 11:6*). God wants us to seek Him diligently. God wants us to pray fervently and earnestly (*James 5:16-17*).

Prayer is supposed to be passionate. Prayer was never meant to be strategic and calculated. God wants you to pour out your heart before Him, even if you don't make sense. Read the Psalms and you'll see how the psalmists prayed. Sometimes there was no structure, they just cried out. Crying is never pretty. Don't try to be too strategic and formal in your prayers. Just cry out to God in humility and desperation regardless of how ugly it is. God is moved by those kinds of prayers.

But don't murmur

We know that in the Old Testament, God was angry with the nation of Israel because they constantly murmured against Him. Someone may ask, what is the difference between murmuring and asking God for the same thing over and over? That is a very good question. There is a lot of similarity between praying persistently and murmuring. Both are persistent. Both involve asking for the same things over and over. Both could be annoying to the one listening. But there is a key difference.

Persistent faith is humble before God and trusts in God implicitly. Murmuring is based on anger and resentment against God. Are you praying out of dependence on God and humility before Him, or are you complaining out of bitterness against God? That is the difference between murmuring and being persistent in prayer.

The children of Israel typically murmured against God whenever something did not go their way. They did not get water, or they were getting the same boring old manna day after day after day. Then they went on and on about how great things were in Egypt. Essentially they were nagging at God. Murmuring is not based on faith and trust in God, but rather animosity against God. Murmuring acts as though God owes you something, faith trusts in God to do what is best.

Wherefore didst thou laugh Sarah?

We all know that Sarah laughed when she overheard God promising Abraham a child, and God confronted her on it.

Therefore Sarah laughed within herself, saying, "After I have grown old, shall I have pleasure, my lord being old also?" And the Lord said to Abraham, "Why did Sarah laugh? ... But Sarah denied it, saying, "I did not laugh," for she was afraid. And He said, "No, but you did laugh!" (Genesis 18:12-15)

But do you know that Abraham also laughed on a different occasion?

Then Abraham fell on his face and laughed, and said in his heart, "Shall a child be born to a man who is one hundred years old? And shall Sarah, who is ninety years old, bear a child?" ... (Genesis 17:17)

Why did God rebuke Sarah but not Abraham when they both laughed for exactly the same thing? In fact, Sarah only laughed to herself, whereas Abraham laughed out loud. Abraham fell on the floor laughing – literally LOL and ROFL. You would think that Abraham's laugh would have been more offensive to God. But that was not the case.

Sarah laughed in derision. Abraham laughed in disbelief (not unbelief). Sarah laughed out of bitterness and resentment against God. Sarah's was a laugh of murmuring. As long as you are not coming from a place of resentment and bitterness against God, you can cry out to Him, reason with Him, argue with Him. Abraham was negotiating with God and offering Him what he thought was a better solution. Go ahead and do that. *"God if I were you, I would do so many things differently."* There is nothing wrong with arguing with God. Sometimes God wants you to pray in an emotional manner. But at the end of the day, remember who is God and who is man. Allow God to show you His ways, and humbly submit to Him. It is possible to pray persistently and passionately without murmuring.

Why God wants us to persevere

So why is it so important to God that we persevere in prayer? Does God get some kind of ego boost out of it? Is God just playing hard to get? These are very valid questions, and as cliché as the answer may sound, God actually wants to develop character in us.

However you feel about President Donald Trump, it is hard to deny the fact that he is a very good parent. If I had a net worth of $4 billion, I would probably spend the rest of my life on a hammock in Hawaii. But even though the Trump family is financially secure for generations to come, and even though his kids did not have to work a day in their lives, he still ensured that he taught them a very strong work ethic. He pushed them so hard, that his daughter Ivanka confessed that even after she was grown up, she could not sleep in on a Saturday morning without feeling guilty.

Why doesn't God just give us what we want? Why does it always have to be such a struggle? I'll tell you why. It's the worst of the worst parents who give their kids everything they want. Good parents realize that even though it is easy sometimes to give kids what they want, kids do not always know best. Sometimes, kids need to learn to work for what they want in order to truly appreciate it.

When I was 12 years old, I wanted an exercise bike, but we could not afford it. So I decided to take matters into my own hands. I asked my parents for a portion of a school grant that was given to us by the government for school expenses. I went to the town center and I bought a number of low priced trinkets that I thought people in my village would like – earrings, crayons, coloring books and the like. I gave it to my aunt who ran the local post office knowing that people would pass there every day to collect their mail.

People purchased my products. I reinvested the profits in more supplies, and I made more money. Eventually I had earned the money for the bike and I was able to return the grant money I had borrowed. What normally happens to exercise equipment? They end up under the bed or in a junk room. That was not the case with me. I used my exercise bike almost every day for 7 years until I left home to go to university. When you have to work and struggle for something, you appreciate it more.

God is our Heavenly Father

As a good parent God wants to bless us with nice things. But more so, He wants to develop godly character and characteristics in us. He wants us to hunger and thirst. He wants us to seek Him diligently. He does not want to make everything easy for us. In fact, God never intended to make Christianity easy. He told the apostle Paul *"Come and I will show you the things you must suffer for my sake" (Acts 9:16)*. God promised that the next life would be easy, not this one.

I am truly sorry that those who propagate the prosperity gospel have led you to believe that Christians are supposed to live in abundance in this life. That is not what the Bible says. This teaching is based on people imposing their own meaning on John 10:10.

> *The thief does not come except to steal, and to kill, and to destroy. I have come that they may have life, and that they may have it more abundantly ... (John 10:10)*

In the verses leading up to this scripture, Jesus noted that all who came before Him were thieves and robbers *(John 10:8)*, and a thief's intention is to steal from the sheep, and to kill and destroy them. He was not talking about the devil, but human teachers who exploited God's people. In stark contrast, He is the good Shepherd who came to give abundant life. Abundant life is simply the opposite of exploitation. Jesus did not come to selfishly exploit people, but to selflessly give Himself so they could have life. It's ironic that this scripture is proclaiming deliverance <u>from</u> the very people who twist it to impose their own understanding of abundant life.

Sure I would love to make a lot of money, but that is not something God has promised in His Word. More importantly, it is not something that is as highly valued by God as you think. God deliberately did not call the mighty *(1 Corinthians 1:26)*, but instead chose the poor of this world to be rich in faith *(James 2:5)*. Jesus turned away the rich young ruler much to the chagrin of His disciples. Our focus should be on laying treasure in heaven *(Matthew 6:20)*. In spite of the trials and difficulties, and even though we may think at times that God is against us, He expects us to persevere and fight through.

> *We must through many tribulations enter the kingdom of God ... (Acts 14:22)*

Speaking of the prosperity gospel, the next chapter examines another myth that also reduces God to a principle – sow a seed and you will be blessed.

CHAPTER 16

SOW A SEED, ANY SEED, ACT NOW!

The last chapter introduced the myth that God is some kind of principle that must be tapped in to. As a result, people who believe it tend to change the way they pray with every new wind that blows.

There is another related myth with which you might be acquainted – sow a seed into the fertile soil of this ministry and God will multiply your seed 100-fold. I refer to this as sow-a-seed-ology. This myth gives the impression that there is some law in the universe that if you give, you will attract blessings. They believe that God is obligated to that law. Many celebrity preachers have taken advantage of this to get their followers to support their extravagant lifestyles. You don't have to live holy or confess your sins. Just sow a seed, and that cancels out everything else. The ubiquity of this doctrine is sickening.

Here is a riddle for you. Some time ago, one famous preacher encouraged his followers that they would receive 7 miracles in 7 days if they sowed a seed of $700. Can you guess what year it was? You got it. It was 2007. Isn't it amazing how God's timing coincides so precisely with our Gregorian calendar?

I understand that Christian media costs money. But look at the lifestyles of the persons who persistently bombard you with sow-a-seed requests. Look at all the private jets, luxury vehicles and multi-million dollar mansions that they have amassed. It is clear that their ministry needs are more than being met. I am not telling you to stop giving. I am simply inviting you to look at their lifestyles, and to exercise wisdom in your giving.

I know of another ~~profit~~ prophet who was invited to preach at a church. After his message, he invited the audience to the altar to receive a *"financial anointing"*. But they needed to come with their seed (*money*) in their hand. Those with $1000 were sent to one section, those with $500 to another section, and those with $100 to yet another section of the prayer line. He ensured that he prayed personally for those with $100 and up as he collected their offering. Then he left! He did not even bother to pray for those with lower amounts. Of course, the ushers collected the money anyway from the less worthy people.

You might be thinking *"Oh that is so awful, I feel really sorry for those poor people."* I don't. I think it is good it happened. I am glad. This way, the blatancy of this scam can finally get through people's resistance. Christians love to defend their pet preachers, even when they are so obscenely unscriptural in their practices and behavior. The real problem is not these conmen who are using Christian pulpits to scam Christians. It is Christians who are so easily scammed. That is the real problem. Christians are obviously not being taught how to discern truth from error.

Deep down inside, these Christians see God as some kind of principle that we can tap into once we have the right formula. This formula may be a new way to pray that has eluded Christians for centuries, or the right person to give money to. Sow-a-seed-ology is just another formula to get stuff from God by reducing Him to an impersonal principle. Whatever the form it takes, it is a myth that keeps Christians in bondage.

How to make soup from a stone

When I was a child, I read a story about a man who showed up in town one day where he met one of the ladies from the town.

> *"Excuse me fine lady, I have travelled all over the world and I have come to teach you how to make soup from a stone", he promised her holding up a single stone. Fascinated, the lady obliged and invited him to her home. He placed the stone very gently in a pot, filled it with water, and put it on the stove.*
>
> *He then asked her, "Do you prefer your soup salty or bland?" "Salty" she replied. "Then add some salt to the water", he instructed her. "If you want to add some more flavor to the soup, why don't you cut a few tomatoes or carrots and add them in?" So she added some tomatoes and carrots. "Are you a vegetarian? Then what are you waiting for? Shred some chicken and throw it in." This she did enthusiastically as the aroma of magic soup quickly engulfed the kitchen.* [16]

This continued until he added all the ingredients that are normally used to make soup, and magically he created soup from a stone. The story ends with the lady finally realizing that he conned her into making soup for him, at which point, she chased him out of her house and threw the stone at him. This is the only part of the story that is different from sow-a-seed-ology – Christians rarely ever recognize that they are being scammed.

How to get blessed the Biblical way

There are many Christians trying to make soup from a stone. They are trying to achieve financial blessings by following some formula they learned on TV. *"Give to this ministry and God will bless you."* Like the lady in the story above, they fail to realize that these pulpiteers are just conmen trying to get their money. Think about it. How they got rich (*by people giving to them*) is different from how they are promising you can get rich (*by you giving to them*). Why is there never a scenario where they give their money to you? Don't they want to be blessed too?

Financial success is wonderful. It is true that the prosperity gospel has given money a bad name. But money is not the root of all evil, the love of money is (*1 Timothy 6:10*). Money only becomes a problem when it becomes our master. We cannot serve God and mammon (*Matthew 6:24*).

The Bible does teach us a lot about financial prosperity, but it is not as simplistic as sowing and reaping. Sow-a-seed-ology is like trying to make soup from a stone. It does not work. The only way to achieve financial success is to add all the ingredients that the Bible outlines. Here is the ingredient list.

Work diligently and don't be lazy.

A little sleep, a little slumber, a little folding of the hands to sleep - So shall your poverty come on you like a prowler ... (Proverbs 6:10-11; 24:33-34)

He who has a slack hand becomes poor, but the hand of the diligent makes rich ... (Proverbs 10:4)

The hand of the diligent will rule, But the lazy man will be put to forced labor ... (Proverbs 12:24)

The soul of a lazy man desires, and has nothing; but the soul of the diligent shall be made rich ... (Proverbs 13:4)

The plans of the diligent lead surely to plenty, but those of everyone who is hasty, surely to poverty ... (Proverbs 21:5)

If anyone will not work, neither shall he eat ... (2 Thessalonians 3:10)

Invest wisely and save your money.

Invest in seven ventures, yes, in eight; you do not know what disaster may come upon the land ... (Ecclesiastes 11:2, NIV)

My son, if you have put up security for your neighbor ... you have been ... ensnared by the words of your mouth ... (Proverbs 6:1-2, NIV)

He who gathers in summer is a wise son; He who sleeps in harvest is a son who causes shame ... (Proverbs 10:5)

Be careful with whom you associate.

He who walks with wise men will be wise, But the companion of fools will be destroyed ... (Proverbs 13:20)

Go from the presence of a foolish man, when you do not perceive in him the lips of knowledge ... (Proverbs 14:7)

Moderate your desire to get rich and don't be greedy.

An inheritance gained hastily at the beginning will not be blessed at the end ... (Proverbs 20:21)

Will you set your eyes on that which is not? For riches certainly make themselves wings; they fly away like an eagle toward heaven ... (Proverbs 23:5)

But those who desire to be rich fall into temptation and a snare, and into many foolish and harmful lusts which drown men in destruction and perdition ... (1 Timothy 6:9)

Give to support God's work (not the devil's work, not man's work).

Let him who is taught the word share in all good things with him who teaches ... (Galatians 6:6)

Let the elders who rule well be counted worthy of double honor, especially those who labor in the word and doctrine. For the Scripture says, "You shall not muzzle an ox while it treads out the grain," and, "The laborer is worthy of his wages." ... (1 Timothy 5:17-18)

Be generous to the poor. God rewards generosity.

He who has pity on the poor lends to the Lord, and He will pay back what he has given ... (Proverbs 19:17)

He who oppresses the poor to increase his riches, And he who gives to the rich, will surely come to poverty ... (Proverbs 22:16)

He who sows sparingly will also reap sparingly, and he who sows bountifully will also reap bountifully. So let each one give as he purposes in his heart, not grudgingly or of necessity; for God loves a cheerful giver. And God is able to make all grace abound toward you, that you, always having all sufficiency in all things, may have an abundance for every good work ... (2 Corinthians 9:6-8)

Don't be dishonest.

Wealth gained by dishonesty will be diminished, But he who gathers by labor will increase ... (Proverbs 13:11)

A good name is to be chosen rather than great riches ... (Proverbs 22:1)

You shall not cheat your neighbor, nor rob him. The wages of him who is hired shall not remain with you all night until morning. ... (Leviticus 19:13)

Render therefore to Caesar the things that are Caesar's, and to God the things that are God's ... (Matthew 22:21)

Submit to God's will

A man's heart plans his way, But the Lord directs his steps ... (Proverbs 16:9)

...you ought to say, "If the Lord wills, we shall live and do this or that." ... (James 4:15)

How Steven worked his way out of poverty

Steven (*not his real name*) grew up as the middle child in a family of seven children born to a farmer and a housewife (*this was before housewives got upgraded to home-makers*). He described their financial status during his childhood as poor to lower middle class.

At age 16, Steven heard the gospel and gave his life to Jesus Christ. Although his parents were heavily involved in a non-Christian religion, they happened to live next door to a church that was active in evangelism. At the time, the church was a dilapidated wooden structure that looked far from impressive, but was full of the power of God. Quite a few of Steven's siblings were also touched by the power of God when they heard the gospel of Jesus Christ. Today, two of them are pastors.

Around the same time, Steven graduated from high school. He could not afford to go to university, so he sought to find a job. He searched for three years. During this time, he assisted his father with planting and selling of agricultural crops to earn a living. It was not luxurious, but it was hard honest work.

At age 19, Steven applied for a job at the local oil company, and by the grace of God he was successful. He credits nothing but the favor of God for him getting that job. This was a company that was heavily political and it was next to impossible to get a job there unless you knew someone. In fact the application form specifically asked if you have relatives in the company. Steven had no contacts. All he had was the favor of God, but that was enough.

Over time, God blessed him with a wife and 3 children. He was able to build a nice home for his family. But then he felt God stir within him a desire to start his own business. Other than his parents' "gardening business", Steven had no business experience. He did not even have a lot to invest in a start-up business. He had $40,000 Trinidad dollars (*approximately US $6,000*) to invest. This was not a lot for a business investment, but it was all Steven had. He went all in.

The first year was tough. Yet he never worried. His faith remained strong. The second year was even tougher. But by the 3rd year, his business saw an exponential growth, and today he makes back his initial investment in a single transaction. I was particularly fascinated with Steven's story because he was not the typical business-man born into privilege. He does not have an MBA or any university degree. He had no contacts, and his family was poor. All he had was the favor of God and a rock-solid commitment to Christ. I asked him how he applied the principles of the scripture to help him succeed in business.

Giving to the Lord's work

Steven believes in giving to the Lord – giving of your time and your substance. Even when he was gardening, he believed in tithing 10% of his income to the Lord. In addition to that, he was very generous in giving to help the church with any outreach endeavor. In fact, he was instrumental in helping to build the wooden church into the nice building that it is today.

Giving to the poor

He is a strong believer in giving to the poor, because he who gives to the poor lends to the Lord. Even in his business, if he can verify that some of his customers are truly needy, he will arrange for them to get supplies at a discounted rate, sometimes free of charge. He estimates that 20% of his income goes into giving to the Lord and the poor.

Giving of his time

He also believes in giving of his time. During his younger years, he devoted a lot of time to attending church services, Sunday School, and crusades. He devoted a lot of his personal time to physically building the church. He believed in consistently giving of his time and substance even when the going got tough. He is a living testimony of the scripture, *"whoever is faithful with little will be entrusted with much"*.

Hard work

Steven works hard. Even before he started his business he found himself working 60-hour work weeks at his job. Today he runs a very successful business to which he devotes 80 hours a week. He sleeps 6 hours a night. He does not have a lot of time to waste watching TV.

Family time

In spite of all of this he makes time to spend with his family. He considers his family time over dinner to be one of his favorite pastimes.

Relaxation

For stress relief, he goes on YouTube to watch sermons and listen to worship music.

Fair treatment of employees

Steven believes in treating his employees well. Even though he is technically a small-business owner, he provides medical benefits to his employees, which is unheard of in his industry. He provides employment to many Christians in his church, but he does not make Christianity a requirement for being employed at his company. He also hires non-Christians with the hope that they would hear the gospel at some point.

What I found interesting about Steven's story is that it went way beyond sow-a-seed-ology. Being generous was just one of many Biblical principles he applied. He was not deceived into thinking all he had to do was give money to a preacher. And he certainly did not think that sowing a seed was an excuse to live unholy and to be lazy. He applied Biblical principles, but he did not treat God as a principle. That is worth repeating. There are principles taught in the Bible, but God is not one of them. Steven worked hard. His faith was strong and his commitment to God was unwavering. He was also very generous in his giving. He is a great example of what a simple Christian with humble beginnings can accomplish through faith in Jesus Christ.

CONCLUSION

Although this book is subtitled *8 Myths that Keep Christians in Bondage*, we have actually debunked over 35 God-limiting myths, which we sorted into 8 categories. That is a measure of how much deception abounds in the church today. That is a measure of the extent to which Christians have limited the God they serve. That is a measure of how much bondage Christians are living in without realizing it.

Why was Israel so rebellious?

We often wonder how Old Testament Israel could so easily turn away from God over and over when the Law of Moses was so clear on what was right and what was wrong. I'll tell you why. They did <u>not</u> know what the Law said. At some point in their history, the Book of the Law got lost somewhere in the Temple, beneath rubble, and no one knew where it was. They knew it existed. They knew little bits and pieces of what they heard. But they did not know where it was or what it said.

Over the centuries, the people turned to Baal worship. They were not deliberately sinning against God. They honestly did not know the right way to serve God. They were following what their leaders had taught them. They were just doing what they saw everyone else doing. They were ignorant and easy to deceive. It had taken them a grand total of 40 days to convince themselves that a golden calf was the God who delivered them from Egypt. That's human nature. Imagine centuries without knowing what the Law of God said. Baal worship soon became entrenched in their culture. The high places became relics of their religious experience. This was the only spirituality they knew. They were in bondage long before they were taken into captivity in Babylon.

Then arose a king called Josiah. In a long line of wicked kings, Josiah was a breath of fresh air. He loved the Lord and did what was right in the sight of the Lord. During his reign, there was great revival in Jerusalem as he attempted to turn the people back to God. He destroyed the altars of Baal and the high places of idol worship.

One day, while they were cleaning up and doing repairs in the Temple, Hilkiah the priest, found the long-lost Book of the Law that God had given to Moses. They had only heard about this book. They brought it to Josiah and read it in his hearing. When Josiah heard the words that were written in the book, the Bible says that he tore his kingly garments, fell to the floor and wept. Josiah knew they had gone astray, but he had no idea the extent to which they had fallen. Based on what was written in that book, he knew they were in big trouble. Unfortunately for them, it was too late. God had already pronounced judgment against Judah, and no amount of tears was going to reverse it.

What is our excuse?

It is not too late for us. The church is in a bad state. You probably know that there are some people teaching false doctrines and leading people away from Christ, but you have no idea the extent of it. You have no idea how bad it really is. You comfort yourself by saying, *"the gates of hell will not prevail against the church."* That is definitely true, but what you don't realize is that the true church is only a fraction of those who call themselves Christians.

Like Judah in Josiah's era, it is much worse than you think. Too many Christians cannot decipher truth from error because there are so many myths being propagated from the most influential pulpits in the Christian world. Their so-called shepherds have turned a blind eye while the flock has been raped and pillaged by ravenous wolves in sheep's clothing. Christian mythology has quickly become ingrained in our religious culture, while we continue on our merry way in blissful ignorance. We have limited God by the myths we have believed. We are in bondage and don't even realize it, and the devil is laughing all the way to the bank. He is on his way to hell, but he is going to hell happy.

I was also guilty of falling victim to myths at one point. I shared some of the ways I had given in to myths in this book. Like you, I once assumed that Christian TV meant sound doctrine. But I came to realize I was wrong. Deep down I had suspected not all was right with these new teachings, but I thought I was being nitpicky. The more I studied the Word, the more discontented I grew with what I saw and heard.

Then it dawned on me. Paul predicted that there would be myths and deceptions in the last days. Jesus predicted that many of these deceivers would be powerful miracle workers who would deceive the very elect. Paul further warned us that these myth-propagators would be very popular and Christians would flock to them in hordes. I realized that I was not being paranoid. Everyone else was being naïve.

John Dixon, a valued member of our *Bible Issues* Facebook group, also came to a similar realization. As a young minister of the gospel, he was told that he could not preach on Sunday mornings until he developed a *"Sunday morning anointing"*. John quickly wised up and studied the Word of God for himself. He learned there is no such thing as a *"Sunday morning anointing"*. As he wrote on his Facebook page,

> *"This is a man-made doctrine that makes us believe that some individuals are more blessed, more used and more favored by God than the rest of us poor saps. [It is designed to] keep the common, ordinary Christian from thinking that God can empower and use him."*

That was a myth created to keep him down. That was a myth designed to keep him in bondage. But once John learned the truth, he was free.

Perhaps you have given in to myths as well. Perhaps these new teachings have completely altered the way you pray. You probably even think you sound aggressive and warlike when you pray. Have you ever seen a tiger, backed up against a wall, being poked by a stick, hissing and snarling, as his captors attempt to force him into a cage? The tiger is being very aggressive, but he is actually in bondage.

Compare this to a tiger who is hunting in the wild. On the prowl, he quietly crouches in the tall grass, patiently awaiting his moment. Then in one swift motion, he pounces upon his prey. He is smooth, ruthless and efficient. He gets the job done. This method of hunting has not changed in centuries. He does not have to learn any new hunting techniques. It is instinctual.

Would you rather pray like a circus tiger or like a tiger on the prowl? The Word of God has endured for centuries, and will endure forever until infinity. Don't change the way the Bible has taught us to pray because of new teachings that are nothing more than God-limiting myths. Once the Word is engrafted in your mind, you will instinctively pray the way you are supposed to.

After reading this book, perhaps you realize that there are areas where you may have given in to myths. Maybe you could now clearly identify and precisely articulate what myth you have believed, why it is wrong, and how it keeps you in bondage. Once you know that, you can then easily find the truth that sets you free.

It was too late for Josiah, but it is not too late for us. How we wish that Christians everywhere could rise up and abandon the God-limiting myths that keep us in bondage. Our dream is to see a church that is so grounded in the truth of God's Word that Christians can easily spot God-limiting myths when they hear it. Our dream is a church where Christians no long run headlong into the next new thing that comes along – like children being tossed to and fro by the trickery of cunning conmen. This was also the dream of the Apostle Paul *(Ephesians 4:13-14)*. We pray that God will use this book to lead many Christians back to the truth, strengthen their faith, and prevent others from falling into error.

Let God be magnified

Let me ask you one final question that I asked at the beginning. Would you go to war with a weapon that your enemy gave you? Then why are we engaging in a spiritual warfare using myths that are not found in scripture?

I invite you to abandon all these questionable new teachings and get back to the Word of God. Abandon these myths that limit God. Abandon these deceptions that were planted by the devil to sidetrack the church into fighting a misguided warfare. Don't let the devil cause you to pray amiss and make your prayers ineffective.

We serve a big God. I know that no Christian will consciously disagree with that. But with your actions, you have limited God. By your prayers, you have limited God and made Him small. The psalmist David declared the bigness of his God:

> *Be exalted, O God, above the heavens; Let Your glory be above all the earth ... (Psalm 57:5)*

> *Let God arise, Let His enemies be scattered ... (Psalm 68:1)*

> *Let those who love Your salvation say continually, "Let God be magnified!" ... (Psalm 70:4)*

I pray that God will not just be magnified in your mind and words, but in your actions as well. Don't just say God is magnified. Act like it. Pray like it. I pray that *"small devil, BIG GOD"* will be for you, more than just a Bible study. I pray that it will be real life. I pray that you will experience it. Let the truth of God's Word be your standard, and may it set you free.

REFERENCES

[1] Elizabeth A. Nixon (2014), *"Are You Decreeing and Declaring in Your Prayers?"*, Charisma Magazine, available at http://www.charismamag.com/spirit/prayer/19877-are-you-decreeing-and-declaring-in-your-prayers [retrieved July 11, 2017].
[2] The Church Guide (2014), *"Prayers, Decrees and Declarations for Breakthroughs, Overcoming and Restoration in 2014"*, available at http://www.thechurchguide.com/prayers-decrees-declaration-2014.htm [retrieved July 11, 2017].
[3] Paraphrased from an unrecorded sermon by an anonymous preacher.
[4] Paraphrased from an unrecorded sermon by an anonymous preacher.
[5] *"Draw Me Nearer"*, words and music by Frances J. Crosby (1875), public domain
[6] Paraphrased from an unrecorded sermon by an anonymous preacher.
[7] A. T. Robertson (1930), *"Word Pictures in the New Testament"*, Baker Book House, Grand Rapids, MI, p. 134; comment on Matthew 16:19.
[8] Paraphrased from an unrecorded sermon by an anonymous preacher.
[9] I Survived …, *"Jennifer/Neely Ann"*, Lifetime Movie Network, 15 May 2011, Television.
[10] *"When We All Get to Heaven"*, words and music by Eliza E. Hewitt (1898), public domain.
[11] *"The Last Mile of the Way"*, words and music by Johnson Oatman (1908), public domain.
[12] Jonathan Edwards (1741), *"Sinners in the Hands on an Angry God"*, available at https://www.blueletterbible.org/Comm/edwards_jonathan/Sermons/Sinners.cfm [retrieved July 11, 2017].
[13] Mack Major (2015), *"Hedonism: Destroying Demonic Sexual Strongholds"*, Eden Decoded Incorporated.
[14] Steve Lyston (2017), *"Masturbation Will Pollute Your Mind"*, The Gleaner (May 22, 2017), Kingston, Jamaica.
[15] Paraphrased from an unrecorded sermon by an anonymous preacher.
[16] Paraphrased from Robert Moser (1808), *"The Stone Soup Story"*, The American Magazine of Wit.

Recommended Reading

For a good non-denominational discussion of the fundamentals of the Christian faith:
Robert P. Lightner (1995), *"Handbook of Evangelical Theology"*, Kregel Publications, Grand Rapids, MI.

For an enlightening discussion of the Word of Faith movement by a charismatic author:
D.R. McConnell (2011), *"A Different Gospel"*, Hendrickson Publishers, Peabody, MA.

For a good online Bible study resource:
"Bible Issues", http://www.bibleissues.org

For a good online Bible discussion forum:
"Bible Issues", https://www.facebook.com/groups/bibleissues

ABOUT THE AUTHORS

Dr. Denver Cheddie is Bible teacher and an Ordained Minister in the Church of God (*Headquartered in Cleveland, TN*). He is also an Associate Professor with a PhD in Mechanical Engineering. He holds Masters Degrees in Biblical Studies, Business Administration and Mechanical Engineering.

Indira Rampaul-Cheddie is a prayer warrior who operates in various gifts of the Spirit including healing and the word of knowledge. God uses her to provide comfort through counseling. By profession, she is an attorney-at-law. She holds Masters Degrees in Biblical Studies, Petroleum Law & Policy, and Business Administration.

We have been married since December 2010, and we share a vision to see the Body of Christ free from myths that have kept Christians in bondage for far too long. We believe that the Bible has answers, whether directly or indirectly, for every situation Christians may face. We use the Word of God and spiritual gifts to counsel people from all over the world, who face problems that they cannot take to others around them, and who are seeking answers they cannot find elsewhere.

Check out also our YouTube channel and our website for more Biblical answers to difficult questions.

www.youtube.com/channel/UC4Wg5aFYx4LdBoLbvoiNtrw
(or search for "Denver Cheddie" within YouTube)

www.bibleissues.org

POST A REVIEW

We pray that this book has been a blessing to you. It will help us a long way if you posted a review. It does not have to be an elaborate review. If you have specific things to say, by all means do so. But reviews could also be very simple like, "Great book", "Highly recommended", "It has been a tremendous blessing to me." Even if you hated the book and you would like to put a negative review, even that is welcome.

You need to go to the same page where you purchased the book and post your review. You can use the link below to get to your review page. Thank you and may God give you the desires of your heart.

www.amazon.com/dp/1979119538/

ALSO IN THE 8 MYTHS SERIES

A Biblical action plan for single Christians looking for a husband or wife

www.amazon.com/dp/1721137505/

FREE E-BOOK on Spiritual Warfare and the Armor of God

www.amazon.com/dp/B07MJT6XVL/

Made in United States
Troutdale, OR
03/28/2025